Unplugging
Power
Struggles

Resolving Emotional Battles with Your Kids
Ages 2 to 10

Jan Faull, M.Ed.

Parenting Press, Inc.
Seattle, Washington

Copyright © 2000 by Janice Faull

All rights reserved. No part of this book may be reproduced in any form without permission from Parenting Press, Inc.

Printed in the United States of America

Designed by Margarite Hargrave Design
Cover and internal illustrations by Mits Katayama

Library of Congress Cataloging-in-Publication Data

Faull, Jan.
    Unplugging power struggles : resolving
    emotional battles with your kids, ages 2 to 10 /
    Jan Faull.
        p. cm.
    Includes bibliographic references and index.
    ISBN 1-884734-43-X (lib. bdg.) –
    ISBN 1-884734-42-1 (pbk.)
        1. Parent and child. 2. Child psychology.
        I. Title.

    HQ755.85 .F398 2000
    306.874–dc21   00-038509

For a complete cataloque of Parenting Press books, call 800-992-6657 or write to us at the address below or visit our website at *www.ParentingPress.com*

Parenting Press, Inc.
P.O. Box 75267
Seattle, Washington 98125

Dedicated to Hallie, Katie, Reisha and
Steve Holton

◆

*It's all about big people helping little people
so they can be big themselves someday.*

Acknowledgments

With love and thanks to —

My husband, Gary, of 31 years, who diligently parented our children while I was out helping other mothers and fathers parent their children,

My three children, Anna, Jerry, and Alan, who each provided me with real-life experience and stories that give this book validity and life,

My friends, including my sisters, who listened faithfully to the ups and downs of getting this book into print,

My colleagues, who validated the thesis put forth in this power struggle information, and

My soul mate.

Contents

Introduction

When my daughter, Anna, was 10 years old, I had been teaching parent education for five years. I thought I knew all the ropes, particularly how to discipline effectively while building a child's self-esteem. Nevertheless, my daughter and I were battling about everything from what she wore to school to how she managed her bedroom and her homework.

I was the determined, powerful parent who wanted to control her life. After all, I had lived longer, was more experienced, and was ultimately responsible for her upbringing. Anna, at age 10, was pushing to take more control of her life, so the two of us engaged in battle after battle, our relationship deteriorating.

Finally, I did some reading outside child development and behavior guidance to understand power struggles that occurred between adults. The book that offered the most insights was *Beyond the Power Struggle* by Nancy Campbell, Ph.D., unfortunately now out of print. Reading this book made me realize that I was not having disciplinary problems with Anna. Instead, we were locked in emotional battles over who was in control.

From the situation with my daughter and from what I have learned working with hundreds of parents since then comes this book. I hope it will help you understand the dynamics of turning power and control over to your children gradually, thereby avoiding power struggles. And if you find yourself engaged in power struggles, here are strategies for resolving them respectfully and reasonably, maintaining dignity for both of you.

Anna is grown up now, we both survived, and our relationship is strong. May this book make parenting for *you* easier and more enjoyable by helping you to avoid or resolve power struggles along the way.

1

The Dreaded Power Struggle

Power struggles are emotional battles between parents and children over who is in control. At some time in your parenting career you've most likely been in a power struggle with one or all of your children.

It's important to realize that a natural tension exists between parents and children. Your job is to teach, train, and influence, to keep your children safe and healthy, teach them values, and guide them until they're old enough to guide themselves. Children, on the other hand, are inclined toward independence; they wish to supervise themselves. The natural tension between these two positions can result in an emotional battle of wills that is a power struggle.

What a Power Struggle Looks Like

A power struggle might occur when you insist your toddler eat her peas and she refuses; or when you're hurrying to get out the door on time each morning and your preschooler dawdles instead of getting dressed.

Power struggles don't always involve screaming and yelling. In some households, they play out with clenched teeth instead of raised voices. For example, Mom might say, "You don't need that swimming suit." Son responds, "Yes, I do. You don't know what I need." A low level of agitation persists, keeping both parent and child tense. And in some families, power struggles are more like a cold war where parties covertly manipulate each other daily. "You can't go to your soccer game until your room is tidy," says Mom. Her child feels controlled, so two minutes before it's time to head out the door, he stuffs all the clutter strewn around his room under his bed and into the closet.

There are many ways to encourage children to eat foods that don't immediately appeal to them. There are lots of approaches for getting children ready for school so you won't be late for work. There are ways to manage children's purchases to satisfy both parent and child. If any of these issues, however, escalates into an emotional power struggle, neither you nor your child will emerge a winner, and the struggle often damages your relationship.

Why Power Struggles Happen

Power struggles baffle parents. Why can't a child simply comply? It would make life so much easier. There are several reasons.

Child's rush for independence. In a power struggle, tension mounts because you want to control your child's behavior at the same time your child wants to be under his own control—proving he's a separate and independent person. Parents almost always have their child's best interest in mind, but even so, a child may not comply simply to prove, "You can't make me do it; I'm the boss of myself." A power struggle over brushing teeth illustrates such a battle ground: the parent, fearing decay, insists on brushing the child's teeth, but the child refuses to open his mouth.

Parent's need for control. No parents want to thwart their child's wishes so severely that the child feels he must argue and fight to prove his independence, but that's really what power struggles are all about. Parents usually cheer when children develop new abilities and display skills in areas like feeding and dressing themselves, learning to read, or managing their own homework assignments. But when children push for autonomy and mastery in areas in which parents don't wish to turn over control, then power struggles erupt.

Personality clashes. Sometimes it won't be a situation that triggers a power struggle, but a certain personality. Perhaps one of your children pushes daily for power and control—beyond what's appropriate for her age. She would run the household, and you, if permitted. This child needs steady and increasing bits and pieces of power and control, but at the same time, decisive, strong parents who will set reasonable limits that keep her safe.

Unrealistic expectations. Power struggles often occur when parents have unrealistic expectations regarding their child's behavior. Maybe you expect to be able to take your toddler to a restaurant, but he isn't mature enough to wait patiently for his food, eat with a fork, or wipe his face and hands with a napkin. Consequently, a power struggle erupts.

Fear for safety. Parental fear is at the root of many power struggles. You've always walked your daughter to the bus stop. Now a second grader, she insists on walking the block to the bus stop with her neighborhood pals. You fear for her safety and refuse. An emotional battle erupts. Your child's push for a new level of independence collides with your need to keep her safe.

Desire to maintain control. Another kind of power struggle starts with the belief, "You're not going to get away with this." Parental fear is again behind the power struggle. You fear if your child gets away with not cleaning up toys today, he won't comply with a curfew when he's a teenager. The power struggle becomes an arena to establish your control. You operate under the erroneous notion that if you force compliance with a preschooler now, the control you establish will keep your child safely under your thumb through the teen years.

Values conflicts. Some power struggles happen when a child's behavior or wishes conflict with the parent's beliefs or value system. Either consciously or subconsciously every parent has an agenda for what he wants for his child—mannerly conduct, academic excellence, respectful behavior—to name a few. When the parent pushes hard for that agenda and the child won't comply, power struggles emerge.

Parental inexperience. Usually parents don't get into power struggles because they are capricious with power or possess malicious intentions, but simply because they are inexperienced. A first-time parent trying to teach her child to dress herself realizes this simple task has become a daily, unfortunate battle of wills.

The Bicycle Power Struggle

When Mary's six-year-old son, Ryan, rode his bicycle down the street and around the corner where he'd been told not to go, Mary had a discipline situation on her hands. She took his bike away for three days and reviewed with him the established bike-riding boundaries. Ryan accepted the control she exerted, which was reasonable to his age and the area in which they lived; he obeyed the boundary rules. No power struggle was involved.

A power struggle did erupt three years later when Ryan turned nine. His bike-riding boundaries were exactly the same as when he was six. He wanted to prove he was trustworthy and capable of traveling beyond the confines of his own street, but Mary wouldn't allow it. She was afraid of what might happen and was bent on keeping him perfectly safe. Ryan still was not permitted to ride beyond their street.

Daily, Ryan bugged his mom, "Please, please let me ride around the block, just once." Mary feared that if she let him go cruising around the block one day, the next he would be begging to ride to the park, and then before long, he'd be pressuring her to ride to the shopping mall.

Ryan's internal developmental time clock was nudging him to take more command of his life. He was ready to take on more responsibility—satisfying his need for adventure and independence—but Mary's fears kept her from letting him go.

She worried a stranger would lure him into his car. She was scared a teenaged driver would roar up the street without watching for children on bicycles. She was frightened about exposing her son to the hazards of the world, so she tried to convince him that, as a responsible parent, she couldn't allow him to ride beyond the established boundaries.

The pitch of emotions escalated. Rather than simply begging and pleading for a bike ride around the block, Ryan cried and threw fits. Frustrated with this behavior, Mary yelled and screamed to make her point. This routine took place daily and left both parent and child emotional and exhausted.

Mary and Ryan were clearly locked in a full-blown power struggle. Mary was struggling to keep her son safe and her control intact; Ryan was fighting to take more control of his life—his personal sense of competency and independence on the line.

Elements of this power struggle:

1. Ryan's natural developmental drive urged him to take more control of his life, solidifying a new level of independence and self-esteem.

2. Mary didn't want to give up control, fearing if she did, her son would demand more and more.
3. Mary feared that if she allowed Ryan to travel the neighborhood on his bicycle, something terrible would happen.
4. A strong show of emotions left Mary and Ryan both emotional and exhausted with no resolution.
5. Mary's attempts to convince Ryan again and again of the validity of her point of view failed. Ryan remaining unconvinced.
6. The power struggle repeated itself, becoming embedded in the daily routine.
7. The parent-child relationship deteriorated.

How to Identify a Power Struggle
You know that you're having a power struggle when:
▶ Your child does not accept your discipline.
▶ The conflict or subject comes up again and again.
▶ Emotions run high.
▶ The parent-child relationship slowly deteriorates.
▶ The issue is never resolved.

Options for Ending the Bicycle Power Struggle

Whatever form the power struggle takes, it is your responsibility to take action to resolve it. There are two key elements for ending any power struggle: a plan, coupled with a matter-of-fact attitude. Without a plan, the power struggle will continue to repeat itself daily. Without a calm demeanor, the plan will fail because emotions fuel the power struggle.

When you need to resolve a power struggle, you always have three options: Hold on; compromise, offer choices, and negotiate; or let go. Sometimes it's important and necessary to hold onto your control; sometimes you'll turn some power over to your child by negotiating, compromising, and offering choices; other times you let go and drop out, or at least drop back. Considering these three options helps you switch from an emotional response of fear and frustration to a problem-solving mode; you can develop a well thought-out plan and execute it—and end the power struggle. Since each power struggle is unique, each one deserves this attention.

Mary has these three options:

1. Hold on. Let's say Mary lives in an extremely dangerous area of town. In this case, it would be appropriate for her to stand firm. Each time Ryan brings up the topic of roaming the neighborhood on his bicycle, Mary can respond in a monotone voice, "You may not ride your bike off our street" or, "What's the rule regarding bicycle boundaries?" That's all, nothing more. She's already explained the situation, she's already given her reasons; there's no need to talk more.

   If Mary takes this hard-line stance, it's important for her to find other opportunities where Ryan can more safely satisfy his need for adventure away from his parents—a need that often crops up in the middle elementary years. Maybe he can learn to take the city bus to a movie theater with a friend. Possibly, Mary can take Ryan and a friend to a safe bike trail for them to go on a long-distance trek. In so doing, she's protecting her son from the hazards of their neighborhood, but meeting his developmental need to take more responsibility and strike out on his own.

2. Negotiate, compromise, offer choices. If she takes this option, Mary can compromise by allowing Ryan to ride around the neighborhood, but always with a friend. She can also stipulate that she needs to ride around several

times with Ryan, pointing out the hazards of the neighborhood and tips for riding safely.

3. Let go. Mary can exercise this option if she comes to realize her determination to control her child is inappropriate and based on an irrational fear. If Mary chooses to let go, she doesn't just throw up her hands in exasperation and give in. Instead, with dignity, she can explain to Ryan that she's reconsidered her stance and why. She can say she's decided to extend his boundaries and then send him on his way.

Resolution of the Bicycle Power Struggle

After careful consideration, Mary chose to compromise. She extended her son's boundaries but only when he rides with a friend. Ryan was thrilled to ride around the neighborhood and didn't mind the "only with a companion" rule. By doing this, Mary didn't need to worry about Ryan pushing for more adventure and independence immediately. Granting a little power and control at each developmental increment usually satisfies the child as well as puts the parent-child relationship back in harmony.

For Mary and Ryan, both parent and child emerged winners; neither overpowered the other with a total win, nor was one forced to completely relinquish his or her position to the other.

The day will come when Ryan will push to ride farther and alone, and then Mary will be forced to reevaluate again. Lying at the root of every power struggle is the natural inclination of children to be under their own power and to control their own lives.

2

Why Children Need Power and Control

Children have the natural tendency to want to direct their own lives—it's imbedded in their drive for self-esteem. You see this determination emerge first at about eighteen months to two years, then it resurfaces again and again in different ways as children grow. For some lucky parents, the gradual transfer of control from parent to child happens with ease and grace; others find themselves in many power struggles as their children push, barge, and bulldoze their way to gain more power and control, working toward independence.

The very words "power" and "control" stir up many emotions and thoughts in parents. One mom's response was, "I don't want my child to hold the power and control in this family. I want it. I see some households where children run the parents, who then tiptoe around, almost fearful of their children." This mom has a legitimate concern. The family situation she's referring to is unhealthy and worrisome because the children have the most power and seem to control their parents. This is obviously detrimental for all concerned.

The healthy course of action for parents is to gradually turn power and control over to children in ways that are appropriate to their child's age and development, while still preserving the family's values and children's safety and health. Children need clear guidance and controls from parents; without them, they struggle aimlessly. Along with that guidance and direction, however, children also need to exercise some control over their own lives.

Power and Control Are Good for Self-Esteem

Offering children choices, permitting and encouraging them to make decisions appropriate to their age and developmental stage, provides them with a personal sense of power and control over themselves and their environment. Your two-year-old can decide whether to sit on the big toilet or the little potty chair to practice toileting. Your preschooler can decide which friend to invite for a play date. Your nine-year-old can decide how to arrange his bedroom.

Never forget, you occupy an automatic position of power over your children. You're stronger emotionally and physically, you're skilled socially, and, of course, you're smarter. You demonstrate this daily to your children by deciding what groceries to buy, preparing food, and managing the family calendar. You work, make and manage money, banking, and credit cards. You can drive a car, navigating busy streets and freeways.

When you allow your preschooler to push the button to open the garage door, you're turning a bit of your control over to her—building her self-confidence and sense of power as you do it. When you allow your son to choose between macaroni and cheese or spaghetti for dinner, you're demonstrating his importance by valuing his opinion. Giving age-appropriate choices is key to effective parenting and a good way to sidestep power struggles.

Think about it this way: if someone were controlling you, constantly telling you what to do, how to dress, how to conduct your household, job, or business, you would be frustrated. You'd say to yourself, "Hey, wait a minute, I'm competent, I can manage some of these decisions on my own. Give me a chance here, will you?" If over-controlled, you might push for control in inappropriate ways, by arguing or giving up. In any case, your self-respect would be threatened. It's not any different for the developing child.

Negative Power and Control

The drive for power and control is so strong in children that if they can't get it in positive ways, they'll seek it in negative ways. Here are five ways this may happen.

Misbehavior. A child who is overpowered and forced to pick up toys without appropriate training and guidance from Mom or Dad may start throwing or breaking the toys instead of complying with your demands. This misbehavior will probably lead to an angry response from you, and your child will gain power by controlling your emotions.

Sabotage. One child, feeling overly controlled by his parents, got back at them by cutting a hole in the side of the detergent box so that the detergent slowly poured out. Another day, this same child took a pin and poked it into the side of the milk container. The family had four children and the parents had a hard time figuring out who was perpetrating the sabotage. The culprit secretly enjoyed the effects of his mischievous activities.

Rebellion. Children can learn the responsibility and gratification of doing homework. If, however, the task becomes a battle of wills between parent and child, the child may rebel against her responsibilities, just to prove, "You can't make me; I alone control my academic progress."

Revenge. If you overpower or inappropriately control a child, she may seek revenge in an area that is particularly important to you. Academic mastery was most critical to Mr. and Mrs. Holbrook. One day their daughter, Kathleen, ripped a precious picture in anger, so Mom and Dad took away television privileges. Kathleen got back at her parents by dawdling through her homework for a week, knowing academics was the aspect of her life her parents valued most.

Over-compliance. Some children whose parents control them too much respond by being unnecessarily compliant. An over-compliant child's self-confidence gradually diminishes when it comes to making decisions that are perfectly appropriate to her age and development. Carrie, at age ten, couldn't decide what to wear to school each morning. Even though she had her child's best interests in mind, by dominating her daughter's every move, Carrie's mother had robbed her daughter of the confidence to make even simple choices and decisions.

Finding the Right Balance

Parents need to strike a balance. Turning too many choices and decisions over to children becomes permissiveness. This is the "Do whatever you like" approach to parenting. It tells children you don't have the interest or energy to care about what they do. You avoid permissiveness by holding onto control in areas of safety and health and dearly held family values. You don't ask your child if he wants to wear a seat belt; it's a safety issue. Children in your family don't choose between watching television before bed or having a story because in your family, story and bedtime go hand-in-hand. Your children need you to muster up the strength to keep them safe, instill your values, and guide them to be responsible, honest, and compassionate people.

When you allow and encourage your children to make some little choices and decisions that are important to them, self-esteem builds at a healthy rate. Then when it comes to complying with big issues involving safety, values, and appropriate conduct, your children will be more cooperative because esteem-building isn't on the line.

The Two-Year-Old

Infants don't know they are individuals separate from their parents; there's an enmeshment of physical and emotional space. Once infants turn into toddlers, the story changes. The toddlers' internal developmental clocks inform them they are separate individuals. Each goes overboard to prove it by saying, "No, I do it my way. Leave me alone!" The parent's job is to understand the child's need for power and control while managing behavior at the same time.

The TV Remote Control Power Struggle

Wesley's parents were desperate to bring their two-year-old son's behavior under control. Almost overnight Wesley turned into a dynamo, running around the house doing what toddlers do best— exploring, experimenting, and touching—trying to understand his environment, learning what impact he had on it, and trying to control it. Jennifer and Mark, his parents, saw Wesley's behavior as naughty. They didn't understand Wesley's behavior was normal for his age. They took it personally, as an affront against them. What happened to the sweet little baby they once knew? He was insistent with demands, persistent with his wants, and would not take "no" for an answer.

More than anything, Wesley was fascinated with the television. He watched Dad and Mom push the buttons on the remote control, fiddle with the cable box, turn the set on and off, and change channels. One minute there would be no picture, the next minute football or sometimes cartoons would appear. Wesley saw how powerful and even magical his parents were and determined to try out the controls for himself. On Super Bowl Sunday, he toddled over, grabbed the remote, pressed the channel changer button and bingo, good-bye "Super Bowl," hello "Sesame Street."

Wesley felt powerful because he could control part of his environment. But it wasn't nearly as exciting as watching Dad leap out of his chair—body rigid, face tense—grab the remote, and yell, "Don't ever touch that remote control again!" At some level, Wesley thought, "You mean all I have to do is touch one of those buttons and I can get my dad to leap and yell? I'm a powerful person. I can control my dad's emotions. This is exhilarating." Now, some children would have been intimidated by Dad's response, but not Wesley. Like many children with his persistent temperament, he liked the power of controlling his dad's emotions.

After that, Wesley tried to manipulate the TV buttons daily. Jennifer and Mark yelled, screamed, and threatened one day; the next day they put him in his crib each time he touched the TV; the next day they just threw up their hands and let Wesley use the remote control anytime he liked. No matter what their approach, Wesley was right back at those TV controls in no time. Then Mom and Dad got scared and thought, "Just how often am I going to have to yell at Wesley to get him to behave?" Fear took over. They projected ahead to the teen years and wondered, "If we don't get Wesley under our control now, how will he behave as a teenager? He'll be a juvenile delinquent plundering the neighborhood, and we won't be able to do anything about it."

His parents couldn't figure out why Wesley didn't respond to their authority. The reason was simple: his curiosity and developmental drive for control and competency were stronger than his desire to please his parents.

Also, at two years old, Wesley had not yet developed the inner restraint to resist something that offered him so much enjoyment. On top of that, he wanted to use the TV as his parents did, mimicking their behavior.

Elements of this power struggle:

1. Jennifer and Mark did not understand Wesley's developmental push for power and control of his environment.
2. Wesley's persistent temperament made him determined to control the TV, despite his parent's wishes.
3. Jennifer and Mark's strong, angry, emotional response doubled Wesley's feeling of power, as he controlled not only the TV, but also their emotions.
4. The discipline approach changed daily, leaving Wesley confused, yet interested, and wondering, "What are Mom and Dad going to do today?"
5. The parents feared that if they didn't get Wesley to stop touching the TV now, he would grow into a delinquent teenager.
6. Because there was no resolution, the power play escalated.
7. The parent-child relationship deteriorated.

Options for Ending the TV Remote Control Power Struggle

So what did Mark and Jennifer do? First, they came to realize that changing plans daily was ineffective and extremely confusing to Wesley. Also, they recognized that their angry response allowed Wesley to gain power in a negative way by controlling their emotions. This only prolonged the power struggle. Mark and Jennifer adopted a matter-of-fact attitude and developed a plan after exploring the following three options.

1. Hold on. They could teach Wesley to stay away from the TV, but if they took this approach, they would need to be perfectly consistent and proceed in exactly the same manner each time Wesley approached it. When he headed toward the TV, they would need to get on their feet, gently pick up Wesley and say firmly, "No! I'm not going to let you touch the TV. You can look at it, but only Mommy and Daddy touch the TV buttons, not Wesley." Then they would move Wesley away and engage him in another activity. In this way, they could provide the self-control that he lacked. They would need to repeat this as many times as necessary. Wesley would quite likely throw a temper tantrum. That's normal when two-year-olds don't get what they want. It would be important for his parents to stay calm if he did this.

If Jennifer and Mark don't want to invest all this effort in keeping Wesley away from the TV, another option is to put it up out of his reach. This way, Mom and Dad would retain control by keeping him from touching the TV at will. This approach would defuse the power struggle. If Jennifer and Mark choose to hold onto control in this area, it will be important for them to provide Wesley with other ways to explore and mimic his parents. For example, they might borrow an unused TV from Grandma. This one will be Wesley's to use; he can satisfy his need to push buttons and copy his parents.

2. Negotiate, compromise, offer choices. A compromise here would be to put the TV up out of Wesley's reach, but then lift him up to push the power button when it was time to turn the TV on or off. With this compromise, Wesley would be getting some of the power he needed as a developing toddler, but in a positive and controlled manner.

3. Let go. Jennifer and Mark could permit Wesley to use the remote and TV buttons as he wishes. If they choose

this option, they would probably find after a few days Wesley would lose his fascination with the TV and move onto something else. If they choose this approach, they might use Wesley's interest in the TV as an opportunity to gradually teach him how and when to use the buttons that magically control it.

Resolution of the TV Remote Control Power Struggle

Jennifer and Mark chose putting the TV up. They would have preferred Wesley simply learn never to touch the TV or remote control, but once they took into account his temperament and age, they knew this was an unrealistic expectation. At two, Wesley simply didn't have the self-control to stay away. When they offered him the opportunity to turn the TV on and off, they saw glee in Wesley's eyes—a sign that self-esteem was building as he learned to control his environment.

Jennifer and Mark did, however, decide to teach Wesley a little self-control. Each evening the family watched a program with the remote control sitting on the coffee table. The rule was: if Wesley touched the remote, he went to his crib for a brief period. Wesley tested this rule only once. After a three-minute stint in his crib, he no longer bothered the remote. He liked being with Mom and Dad for this special time. Jennifer and Mark felt more competent and in control as they established this one rule for Wesley and it dissolved their fears about his future as a delinquent.

Life would be so much easier if children would do as they're told and happily remain under their parents' control. After all, you're the parent, you know what's best, you're experienced in life, you're older and wiser. Rather than being frustrated and threatened by your children's needs to gradually manage themselves, try to realize that the power to self-manage is a key element in every child's self-esteem. This drive lies within every child. You satisfy it most successfully by allowing and even encouraging them to make choices and decisions that are appropriate to their age and development. The tricky part is to discover ways to turn over the controls without jeopardizing their safety or health, or your standards, while teaching them appropriate behavior along the way.

One of the best ways to do this is through choices and decisions but, of course, all parents will struggle from time-to-time about which choices are appropriate for children to make at different ages.

3

Choices and Decisions Suitable for Children

You can minimize or sidestep power struggles when you use the simple technique of offering children choices. You can encourage your kids to make decisions that are appropriate to their age and development. When children make choices, they acquire control and because they have chosen it, they are usually eager to follow through.

When Jeremy chooses milk rather than apple juice for breakfast, he's more likely to drink it because, by making the choice, he's invested in it. If your child chooses basketball over soccer, she'll probably be more willing to participate because she chose the sport herself, instead of you dictating it for her.

But sometimes it's difficult to know which choices and decisions are appropriate for children to make. For first-time parents it can be especially difficult. Today there's even a trend toward offering children too many choices. And sometimes children still don't follow through, even when they've made the choice themselves. For example, your child may choose cereal over pancakes for breakfast, but then demand toast instead. At that point, you may feel exasperated and controlled by your child and blow up.

Instead of losing your temper, step back and decide if

you're going to make the toast or not. You can say, "No toast, you chose cereal today; you can choose toast tomorrow." Of course, you'll take the risk your child will eat nothing and end up being cranky from no breakfast. If, however, you stop there after one choice, your child will eventually learn that when he makes a choice, you will hold him to it.

Choices for Toddlers

Offering toddlers choices can be tricky. If you ask your toddler, "Do you want to wear your boots or shoes?" she'll probably say "shoes" simply because it's the last word she heard. Toddlers are typically indecisive. They don't know what they want; in fact, they want it all. When your toddler can't decide, you must step in and decide for her. Be forewarned though, when it comes to denying or delaying the instant gratification toddlers frequently demand, tantrums are almost inevitable. Your child will survive the emotional explosion and so will you.

Rather than offering toddlers choices regarding "this or that," a concept they really don't understand, just give them some of the control they're demanding. Let them decide which toys they'll put in the bathtub. Allow them to line up all the cars at clean-up time. Let them take two teddy bears to the grocery store. Allow them to pick two bedtime stories. Allow them to pick the shirt they'll wear, even if it's the same one they've worn day after day.

Choices for Older Kids

It's interesting to note that at certain ages, particular issues become paramount to the child. For many preschoolers, it's extremely important to them to choose what they wear. For school-aged children, it's important for them to control when and where they do their homework as they realize it is ultimately their responsibility.

At these times, you need to simply step back or offer choices. You can negotiate or compromise, allowing your child little bits and pieces of power and control appropriate to his age and development. Letting your child hold the reins for certain issues minimizes the chance of power struggles occurring.

When you make a decision for your child, ask yourself, "Is this a decision my child could be making for himself?" If it is, step back and allow your child to make it. Making choices offers your child the opportunity to gain competence. Your child can't acquire confidence when you hold all the controls.

Choices and Decisions for Each Age and Stage

Below is a sketch of appropriate choices children can make as they grow. Although you are handing over some control here, don't ever feel you can't offer your input and advice about the choices you give your children. You can say, "This is how I see the situation," or "Here's what I would do." It's your job to provide guidance and suggestions; you're experienced, older, and wiser. Now read over the choices suitable for children in different age groups. Notice none jeopardize children's safety or a family's values.

Preschoolers. Offer three- to-five-year-olds reasonable choices regarding:
▶ The clothes they wear
▶ Family-approved television programs to watch
▶ Bedtime stories
▶ Who to have over for a play date
▶ What to play with and where

There are so many rules and schedules for preschoolers to follow. Allowing them these choices gives them some say in their own lives. Maybe they can't transform the living room into a fort, but they can use tape and blankets to make a secret camp in their bedroom. They can't color on the walls or furniture, but with paper and colored markers they can decide all on their own what they're going to draw. When it comes to play and creative activities, children need to hold the controls without interference from you.

School-aged children. Children in the middle years can choose:

- ▶ Extracurricular activities such as music, scouts, sports
- ▶ When and where they'll do their homework
- ▶ How to spend their allowance or gift money
- ▶ What kind of hairstyle to wear
- ▶ How to arrange their bedrooms

Children also need to pick and control their own hobbies. If your son likes putting together models, let him control the kind he'll assemble and his pace for progressing from one level of difficulty to the next. Hobbies offer control and competency for the school-aged child.

Five Tips on Giving Choices

Giving a choice within a "no-choice" situation. You don't let your toddler decide whether to sit in her car seat or not. It is a safety issue; she must sit in it. But you can offer a choice within this "no-choice" situation. She can choose to look at a book or play with a small toy once in her car seat.

If going to religious services is part of your family's value system and your children are simply expected to go, there's no choice. But offer your children some choice about what they'll wear and what quiet activities they'll take along to help them remain quiet during the service.

When you must say "no," say "yes" to something else. When you can't offer a choice and you must say "no" to your child, then find somewhere else for the child to hold the controls. Let's say you can't allow your eight-year-old son to go to the park with his friend because it's unsafe. Your child accepts your "no" about going to the park, but later he asks if he can put together a macaroni casserole for dinner. You suspect he'll make a huge mess in the kitchen, nevertheless, you give him the go-ahead. In this way, you satisfy his need for competency without compromising his safety, fulfilling his need for independence thwarted earlier that day.

Children must live with the responsibility of their choices. Your daughter decides to sign up for soccer rather than swimming. You buy the shoes and the uniform. After several weeks of practice, she decides soccer really isn't her sport and besides, she'd rather be on the swim team. Tell her she must live with her decision and stay with soccer for the season.

If you offer your child a choice, make certain you can accept either option. One dad gave his daughter this choice: "You're invited to Sarah's to spend the night. You have a choice. You can clean your room and then go to Sarah's, or you can choose not to clean your room and stay home tonight." Of course, Dad thought his daughter would decide to clean her room and go to her friend's. The daughter felt manipulated. She chose to leave her room messy and remain at home. Dad was shocked and angry. He had given a choice, but was really unwilling to accept one of the options he offered. Dad was manipulating his daughter, not offering a true choice.

Guide children through a series of choices that lead to competency. Ask questions and offer choices that help a child develop a plan to succeed. For example, when school begins you can start your child off on the right foot by asking, "On nights when you have homework, you'll need to decide to do it before or after dinner. Then you'll need to decide if you want to do it at the kitchen table or in your bedroom. On nights when you have lots of assignments, you'll need to decide if you want to work non-stop, or take a break between assignments."

The Dinner Party Power Struggle

Four-year-old Jeremy and his mom Julie engaged in power struggle after power struggle in all the routine parts of the day: getting dressed, fastening the seat belt, going to and leaving the grocery store, and more. Then there were struggles about what to eat and where to sit at breakfast, lunch, and dinner. Problems cropped up again when it was time for bath and bed.

Julie was exhausted, baffled, and ready to give up on parenting. When she was a little girl, if her mom gave her cereal for breakfast, she'd eat it, no questions asked. She expected Jeremy to be as compliant as she was, so when Jeremy flatly refused to eat his cereal, she was overwhelmed. Most days he negatively controlled the household and especially his mother. She responded to Jeremy's behavior by throwing up her hands, pleading with him to cooperate, and then dragging him from one situation to another. This approach didn't do any good; Jeremy's behavior only got worse.

Julie's problems with Jeremy came to a head one evening when she invited guests for dinner. This was to be an adult evening—children not included. Jeremy's parents expected him to keep a low profile; he had other ideas. To be part of the gathering, Jeremy started turning the dining room lights on and off as the adults ate their dinner.

Trying to avoid a scene, his parents gritted their teeth and politely asked Jeremy to stop. He refused to comply and continued to run around turning other lights on and off, laughing as he did so. The irritation level of the guests rose as they tried to hide their aggravation.

The scene ended with Julie dragging Jeremy to his room where he proceeded to throw a royal temper tantrum that everyone heard. She stayed with him for over an hour until he fell asleep. With Jeremy finally out for the night, Julie returned, embarrassed, to her guests.

Elements of this power struggle:

1. Julie did not understand Jeremy's temperament and constant push for control.
2. There was recurring negativity in the daily routines—with no resolution.
3. Julie had unrealistic expectations for Jeremy's age, particularly in situations such as the evening of her dinner party.
4. Jeremy was not getting power and control in positive ways through age-appropriate choices, so he found ways to acquire it negatively through misbehavior.

Resolution of the Dinner Party Power Struggle

Jeremy's parents needed to allow and encourage him to make choices. By allowing some decision-making opportunities, Jeremy could gain a personal sense of power and control in an appropriate way—something every child needs. The dinner party incident was a perfect example of Jeremy getting power in a negative way. He felt powerless and excluded, but he certainly found a way to control the entire evening!

Julie's challenge was to think of ways in each daily

routine to provide Jeremy with opportunities to feel powerful. The plan that worked the best involved an alarm clock.

Jeremy had begged for his very own alarm clock. Julie thought a clock was an inappropriate item for a four-year-old to own, but nevertheless, she decided to grant his wish. Because getting ready for preschool had been such a battle, she decided to drop out of the morning power struggle and turn this control over to Jeremy.

She simply said, "Jeremy, the clock will go off at seven o'clock. You need to get up, get dressed, and come downstairs for breakfast." To set the stage for success, Mom helped Jeremy choose his clothes the night before and lay them out in his bedroom. Jeremy felt important with the responsibility of this new morning routine. He enjoyed handling it on his own—no more problems getting dressed.

Julie supplied Jeremy with more and more opportunities each day for positive control and competency. For example, she let him choose between eggs or cereal for breakfast or which book to read before bed.

Whenever Jeremy made even the slightest choice on his own, his mother tried to recognize and affirm it:

"Jeremy, what a nice looking shirt you picked out today. Good for you."

"Jeremy, you're building with blocks and making an interesting city. I like your ideas."

"Jeremy, you choose the video to watch tonight."

And she continued to offer even more choices:

"Jeremy, tonight is your night to decide what we're having for dinner."

"Would you like to have a friend over to play? Who would you like to have?"

Once Jeremy internalized a feeling of power and control that this kind of decision making provides, Julie was able to relax. Real improvement occurred when Jeremy learned to accept certain "no's." Julie could say,

"No, Jeremy, I know you want to cross the street all by yourself, but I can't allow it, it's not safe. Hold my hand." Jeremy would comply. A month earlier, this situation would have triggered a tantrum.

It was months before his parents chose to entertain again, but when they did, they developed a plan for Jeremy. He was asked to serve appetizers and then invited to watch a video of his choice for the next hour. His mother put him to bed, as always, to maintain his consistent bedtime routine. With this plan, Jeremy's need for attention and control were met, but the adults were still able to have their own evening—children on the sidelines.

Offering your children choices and supporting their need to make decisions appropriate to their ages and abilities is a good way to avoid power struggles, build their self-esteem and sense of competency. Even so, the most skilled and experienced parents can find themselves in power struggles. Once you're stuck in a power struggle with your child, how can you get out of it?

4

Sometimes You Just Have to Hold On

In order to truly resolve a power struggle, it's crucial for each parent to get beyond emotional involvement and develop a plan of action. It's important to keep in mind the three options for resolving power struggles.

1. Hold on. When you exercise this option, you don't waver. Your child may whine, gripe, complain—even throw a temper tantrum—but you remain steadfast. Selecting this option is most appropriate when the issue involves the child's safety or your family's values. If holding onto your power and control provokes your child to hit you or destroy property, you should restrain or contain him in a firm, not harsh, manner.

2. Negotiate, compromise, offer choices. With this option, you turn over a little control to your child through compromise and negotiation, or by offering choices. You choose this option when you sense your child yearns for and is able to take on more responsibility. You realize the child's overall behavior will improve when you allow him some control and then support him as he manages more of his own life.

3. Let go, drop back, drop out. Letting go is appropriate when you realize that by trying to hold on in a situation which you simply can't control, you are losing your ability to influence your child; the power struggle dominates the parent-child relationship. Maybe you realize the push-pull, tug-of-war is a waste of time and energy. You suspect your child really is capable of holding the controls and decide to offer that chance. With dignity, you announce to your child, "I'm dropping back and letting go." The paradox you discover is that when you drop back, often the child miraculously opens up to your influence.

This can be the most difficult option for many to choose because, when you drop out, you may feel like you have lost a part of your influential role as parent.

Hold On When Safety Is the Issue

It's important to realize that in some areas of your parenting life you will more easily share control with your child, whereas in other areas, you might find yourself battling for control.

Debbie always trusted her daughter's handling of academics. When second grader Alice first came home with a homework assignment, Debbie sat by her and provided guidance and support. Gradually, Debbie sensed Alice's interest in taking on more of this responsibility, so she backed off. Debbie always stayed aware of what Alice was learning, but didn't oversee her work on a daily basis. Debbie insisted the television stay off weekday evenings, but other than that she trusted her daughter to manage her academic responsibilities. There was never a homework power struggle in their home. However, a power struggle did erupt when Alice, at age nine, refused to wear a bicycle helmet.

The Bicycle Helmet Power Struggle

Alice simply refused to wear her bicycle helmet. When she climbed on her bicycle without it, Debbie became instantly enraged and began her usual lecture, "Kids fall off bicycles—I read about it all the time in the newspaper. Head injuries cause paralysis. Look at Ben from our old neighborhood—he hit his head on a curb and now he's in a wheelchair for life."

Alice argued back, "I hate that stupid helmet; I look like a geek wearing it. None of my friends wear helmets. I'm not going to fall. It makes my head feel hot. You can't make me wear that thing."

Some days Mom won out. She held onto the bicycle and refused to let Alice ride. Others days she threw up her hands in exasperation, gave up, and her daughter rode away, hair flying in the wind. Other days she bribed Alice, "If you wear your helmet, I'll let you watch 30 minutes of TV tonight."

This bicycle routine continued for weeks. Every time Alice pulled out her bike from the garage, Mom's body turned rigid and tense. She watched Alice out of the corner of her eye to see if this time she'd don her helmet without a fight. Not Alice—each day she mounted her bike and started out, leaving her helmet on the garage floor. Each time, Debbie met her in the driveway, where the arguments happened.

Elements of this power struggle:

1. Debbie became instantly angry when she saw Alice without a helmet. It was exciting for Alice to be in control of her mom's emotions. Debbie's strong emotional response kept the power struggle going.
2. Debbie repeatedly tried to convince Alice of her point of view and failed to acknowledge Alice's dislike of bike helmets.

3. The frequent change of approach and lack of consistency perpetuated the struggle. One day Debbie held on, the next day she attempted a compromise by offering 30 minutes of TV, then other days she dropped out and just let Alice ride with her head unprotected. The change of approach left Alice wondering and interested about what her mother would try next.

4. The bike helmet power struggle became part of Alice and Debbie's daily routine. Children thrive on consistency and routine, even when it's negative. This after-school power struggle made Alice's life predictable.

Resolution of the Bicycle Helmet Power Struggle

Debbie's only option was to hold on. Because this situation involved Alice's safety, Debbie had to determine the best way to hold on to her power and control without further damaging her relationship with her daughter.

Debbie decided to lock up the bike. She first acknowledged her daughter's point of view, "I know you hate wearing your bicycle helmet; it's uncomfortable and you feel like a geek wearing it, nevertheless, as a responsible parent, I simply can't allow you to ride your bike without one. If you fell and injured yourself, I'd never forgive myself. It's because I love you so much. Your bicycle is locked in the storage closet. When you put your helmet on, I'll unlock it."

Of course, Alice threw a temper tantrum, "That's not fair! You're a control freak. I hate you—you're mean!" After this burst of anger, she stomped off to her room and slammed the door, yelling, "I'm never going to ride that stupid bike again! Lock it up forever—see if I care."

Alice was mad not only because Debbie asserted her

power, but because her mother had changed—she no longer participated in the power struggle that had been part of their daily routine for weeks. Children generally do not respond well to change; sometimes they react to it with anger.

Alice's anger was only temporary. Later that afternoon a friend invited her to go on a bike ride. When Alice put on her helmet, Debbie unlocked the bike and the two girls rode off together.

When Alice actually placed her helmet on her head, she had not only decided to keep herself safe, but she accepted Debbie's control. A little part of her own importance and worth as an autonomous person was diminished, but that's expected when the issue is truly over the child's safety. Wisely, Debbie did not gloat or repeat her earlier lectures on bike safety. Instead, she said, "Thanks for wearing your helmet. I'm glad you're keeping yourself safe. I know you don't like wearing that helmet, but thank you for doing it. I trust you'll wear it even when you're out of my sight."

So, what's to stop Alice from chucking her helmet in the bushes once she rounds the corner and then retrieving it on her way home? There would be a big difference between Debbie knowing Alice was doing this and simply worrying about it. If Debbie actually saw Alice riding without her helmet, then she must confront her with the misbehavior and give her a consequence: "I saw you on your bike without a helmet. You won't be allowed to ride your bike for one week." Then she would need to lock up the bike and say no more.

If Debbie suspected her child of this defiant behavior, it's best not to confront her unless she really has some evidence. Debbie need not sneak around following her daughter or calling neighbors to watch for her. She needs to cultivate goodwill, trust, and forthrightness with her child. If she lurks about spying on her, Alice may only become better at hiding misbehavior, creating another kind of struggle and damaging the parent-child relationship further.

Since Alice decided to follow the helmet rule, diminishing her sense of control, it's advisable for Debbie to find other areas for Alice to safely acquire more control. She might allow her and a friend to go to a movie by themselves. She might permit her to ride into the city on a bus for an afternoon adventure. Or she could stretch her bedtime routine from eight thirty to nine o'clock.

Debbie wouldn't do these things as a point of negotiation or as a trade-off. She's not saying, "I made you wear a helmet, so you get to do this instead." She is trying to bring back into balance the degree of power and control between parent and child. She had to force her control in the bike helmet area, so she decides to give it up in another area that seems reasonable and safe for Alice's age and development.

Avoiding the Bicycle Helmet Power Struggle

As you can probably see, this power struggle could have been avoided altogether. The first time Alice took out her bike without her helmet, Debbie should have matter-of-factly refused her the ride by locking up her bike until she placed the helmet on her head. It's easy for other parents to see the solution, but it wasn't so easy for Debbie. Her fear for her daughter's safety quickly triggered her emotions. Unfortunately, when immersed in a power struggle, it's hard to step back and evaluate the effectiveness of your approach.

You can avoid power struggles like Debbie's by establishing rules and habits based on safety and your values. In every family there are non-negotiable safety rules: children *must* sit in car seats, then, later, they must wear seat belts. Parents do not allow children to play with matches. When children are little, they must stay in the backyard when playing outside; as they get older and roam the neighborhood, they must keep parents apprised of their whereabouts.

How to Establish a Safety Rule

Since Debbie could not compromise on her bicycle helmet rule, how could she have used her positive parenting power to instill this safety rule and gain her daughter's co-operation? The best way to instill safety rules, such as a bicycle helmet rule, is in the following manner:

Start young. Place a helmet on the child's head from the very first time she gets on a tricycle.

Be consistent. Watch each time she rides to make sure the helmet goes on and be right there to put the helmet on, if necessary.

Deliver a safety-related message. Say, "This helmet protects your head in case you fall. It's my job to keep you safe."

Model the rule. When you ride your bike, wear a helmet. It's critical to model what you expect from your child.

Cite the law. If there's a bike helmet law in your county, refer to it by saying, "In our county, it's the law: everyone must wear a helmet."

Call attention to a person not following the rule/law. If you see someone without a helmet, you can point out how that person's head is not protected and what might happen if he or she fell.

Cite stories in the media. If you read about or see on television an accident about someone who fell and sustained an injury from not wearing a helmet, call it to your child's attention.

Praise or acknowledge the child when she follows the rule. When your child automatically puts on her bike helmet without a reminder, it's important to say, "You're keeping yourself safe by remembering to wear your helmet. Good for you."

Does this sound like going overboard? It isn't, really. You don't need to shove the point down your child's throat, but if you're really going to instill any safety rule, you must take a deliberate, conscientious approach. You don't just hope or assume your child will wear a helmet consistently because you demand it. During the preschool years, you create a bike helmet habit, then once your child is school-aged, you engage her intellect by explaining the reasons behind the rule. Proceed in a low-key, yet deliberate way.

Even with this consistent and loving approach, a child, especially one with a challenging temperament, may test your rules—not because you're unreasonable, but because she's simply driven internally to do so. It's hard to understand why a child would jeopardize her own safety just for the sake of challenging a parent, but some do. Others resist certain safety and values rules just because they're kids without the maturity, judgment, or life experience to weigh the risks and benefits of their every action.

Instilling Values, Avoiding Power Struggles

Like safety issues, some family values are also non-negotiable. If a family values exercise, then parents might require their children to play sports. If learning is a valued activity, reading before bed is part of the nightly routine rather than a television program. If parents value to-getherness, the family gathered for dinner every night might be a priority for which they set a goal and stick to it as their children grow.

Family dinners were important to the Bernard family. Despite busy schedules and demanding jobs, both parents agreed that as much as possible, the family would dine to-gether. When their children were babies, Mom or Dad would hold each on their laps as they ate. Once in a high chair, the child would sit and eat along with the rest of the family. As preschoolers, the children didn't eat much, but they were required to sit at the table for at least five minutes.

By the time the children reached school age, the dining routine was well established. When asked why eating together was so important, the parents would respond with something like this, "It's the only time in our day when we are able to be together to validate the importance of the family. Everyone's presence counts; each person's contribution is significant. When one member is not able to join the family for dinner, their absence is recognized. When the focus is on conversation and being together, everyone usually eats what they need." The parents were clear and consistent about requiring their children to sit at the table, and once there, each person had a chance to talk, was listened to, and learned that their presence was important and made a difference.

When they become teens, the Bernard children might protest this family value, yet the parents know that since the routine and value are well established, the protest will likely only be temporary and no power struggle will ensue. If the Bernards attempted to establish family dinners when their children turned 10 and 12 years old, the routine would be much more difficult to initiate and a power struggle might follow.

Hold on to Your Control
When Your Child Is Out of Control

Young children lack inner controls. When they can't control themselves, you must step in and provide the control they lack. When it comes to stopping aggressive or violent behavior, you don't negotiate or drop out, you stop the behavior.

When young children are stopped from doing what they want to do or are used to doing, sometimes they act out violently. In a civilized society, parents cannot tolerate violent acts. You must be firm in your approach to ending any hurtful, aggressive behavior.

Many children between the ages of two and five display aggression. A child may respond aggressively when a parent denies her one more cookie, or when a friend grabs a toy out of her hand. The time to teach children to curb their aggressive impulses is when they're little; you can't just hope the child will outgrow this behavior.

If your child hits, kicks, throws objects, or bites, stop him immediately. Say, "I will not let you hurt others," while restraining the child. Remove your child from the scene by gently carrying him to another part of the house or outside. Don't establish eye contact, intense attention that often unintentionally reinforces negative actions.

Stay with your child until he's calm. If he attacks you, you may need to isolate him briefly in a safe place. Realize, however, that your presence often helps your child regain control and calm the feelings of anger and frustration that arise from not having his needs and desires immediately satisfied.

Your approach here isn't harsh—it's clear and deliberate. You want to help your child gain control, not add to the tension of the moment by spanking or yelling. The calmer you are, the more quickly your child will calm down. Let your child know it's your job to keep everyone safe. Remain firm and kind.

Some children are by nature more aggressive than others. Your child might require more energy and involvement from you to end the aggressive acts. No matter what level of aggression your child displays, stay calm and consistent when you intervene. Help your child solve problems without hurting others or destroying property.

Rules

Joe's daughter, Carrie, is only nine years old, but she likes to talk on the telephone non-stop and do her homework in front of the television. So Dad established this rule: No TV or phone between 7 and 8 p.m. on weekdays. When Carrie first heard the rule, she spouted off, "You're not fair. My favorite programs are on between 7 and 8. My friends can't talk after 8 o'clock. This new rule is stupid. You're mean!"

Despite her complaints and arguments, Dad held fast to the rule. He allowed Carrie to record her favorite programs and didn't worry about the missed telephone time. Within three days, Carrie adjusted to the rule; it remained in place through high school. Dad's hard-line approach clearly paid off. Other aspects of Dad's parenting were more relaxed, but the TV and phone interfered with his interest and concern for academics—a value which he held dear.

If you have a clear rule you want to instill, make sure it's reasonable and enforceable. Don't try to instill too many new rules at once. You will almost certainly have to put up with some whining and complaining as your children adjust to the change the new rule brings. If you're clear about what you want, unemotional, and don't expect your children to accept the enforcement of this new rule happily, the rule will eventually become part of your daily life. Establishing rules following this procedure avoids power struggles.

How to Establish a Rule

1. Establish one enforceable rule at a time.
2. State the rule clearly.
3. Use a businesslike tone of voice as you state and restate the rule.
4. Be perfectly consistent in applying the rule.
5. Ignore any irrelevant behavior or arguments.

5

Choices, Negotiation, and Compromise

When you offer choices, compromise differences, and negotiate a dispute to the point of resolution, you are exercising the second option for resolving a power struggle. Here you can hold onto some of your power and control, while turning a portion of it over to your child. Remember, parenting requires the gradual transfer of control from parent to child as the child matures. When you're in the middle of a power struggle, if you can step back, compromise, or negotiate, you will more likely retain a reasonable measure of control, while still defusing the power struggle.

You can use this option in a number of ways:

▶ Offer choices, negotiate, or compromise on-the-fly.
▶ Build bridges to competency by offering a series of choices.
▶ Develop an incentive program providing a choice to work, or not work, for a reward.
▶ Offer choices that lead to different consequences.
▶ Reach a compromise through formal negotiations.

Defusing Power Struggles On-the-Fly

So many power struggles occur unexpectedly, catching you off guard at an inopportune time. When faced with such a power struggle on-the-fly, if you can skillfully shift into offering choices, do a little negotiation, or propose a compromise, you can often avoid a full-blown struggle.

The Shoes Power Struggle

Bill was surprised one Monday morning when five-year-old Sally refused to put her shoes on for preschool. She said, "I'm not going to put my shoes on and I'm not going to preschool." Sally had always gone to school happily. Why the big push for power and control that particular morning?

Who knows? Children have a strong need to be in control, and that morning Sally chose shoes and school to prove herself; she initiated a classic power play. Dad first tried to hold onto his control. He challenged Sally, "You are going to preschool and you're putting on your shoes now." Bill forced Sally into her shoes. Unfortunately, she just kicked them off with an expression that said, "Now, what are you going to do about that?"

Resolution of the Shoes Power Struggle

Dad's impulse was to yell and force Sally into her shoes again. Instead, he stopped and talked to himself, "I'm a competent adult. I can manage this situation calmly. I won't force the issue right now. I'll state my expectations again and then back off." Dad took a deep breath and calmly stated, "We'll be leaving for preschool in ten minutes. You need to put your shoes on." Then he walked away.

Often all that's needed with kids is a little time. Maybe Sally was simply saying, "I won't do what you want right now, but give me a couple of minutes and I might change my mind." But that morning Sally really dug her heels in—after the ten minutes her shoes were still off.

Bill decided to offer Sally a choice of footwear, "You can either wear your boots or your shoes to preschool, you decide." Choices give kids power and control in a situation and often motivate them to go along with your agenda. Unfortunately for Bill, Sally still refused, "I'm not wearing my boots *or* my shoes, no way."

Bill coached himself again, "Okay, I'm running out of options here but I'll offer one more choice." He said to his daughter, "We're leaving for preschool. You can either go with something on your feet or nothing on your feet." Sally didn't move, so he put her and her shoes in the car.

As it turned out, Sally was a little embarrassed to arrive at preschool without her shoes on so once Dad exited the preschool, she quickly slipped them on.

In this situation, Sally and Dad each won an aspect of the power struggle. Dad won because Sally went to preschool as always, and Sally won because she decided whether she was going to wear shoes or not. In any power struggle, it works best if both parties can emerge victorious. Why was this shoe and school business such a big deal to Sally? Why didn't she just put the darn shoes on and hop in the car, as usual? It took so much time, thought, and energy to struggle. Why couldn't she just comply?

Well, Sally was pushing for more power in her life, and that morning she picked shoes and preschool as her arena for testing just how much power and control she could wrest from her dad. Bill successfully used choices and compromise to avoid a power struggle that could have continued for days and become a negative part of the morning routine. Sally discovered she could choose between shoes or no shoes, but not between preschool or no preschool.

Building Bridges to Competency

When young, children don't yet have the ability to think ahead and plan. They're impulsive; they want what they want, when they want it. One task of being a parent is to reduce children's impulsive actions by helping them think through situations before acting. Rather than engaging in a power struggle, parents can help their child by offering a series of choices which build a bridge to resolution, while developing competency at the same time.

The Doll Power Struggle

Grandma traveled to France and brought home a beautiful doll with a hand-painted face for her granddaughter, Kim, age seven. Kim wanted to take the new doll to school. Laura, her mom, warned against it, "The doll might get dirty, damaged, or lost."

Despite her mother's warning, Kim was determined to take her doll to school. A power struggle erupted. Mom was mad, "You don't appreciate the gift. Grandma brought it all the way from France, and now you're taking it to school and risking ruining it. Why can't you just do as I say and leave it at home?"

Kim responded, "It's my doll, I can do anything I want with it." By the end of the evening the doll was stuffed in Kim's backpack ready for school. As Kim stomped off to her bedroom, Mom called, "Just take that doll to school, see if I care! You'd better start thinking how you'll explain to Grandma that your doll got ruined. I should just take the doll and hide it. You're obviously not old enough to care for it properly."

Resolution of the Doll Power Struggle

By morning, Laura didn't feel right about her decision to make Kim face the possible consequences of taking the doll to school. She figured that life provided enough consequences for children without setting them up for failure. Kim never had to protect a precious item going to and from school before. If the doll got scuffed up or damaged, Kim would be upset. Mom wanted to prevent the feelings of failure and guilt Kim would experience if that happened; she decided she'd rather help lay the groundwork for success.

Laura's goal was to build a bridge for Kim that would protect the doll and help her daughter develop experience in caring for a precious object.

Laura approached her daughter differently the next morning, "Kim, I realize you really want to take your doll to school. I've thought it over and I think you're old enough to do this, but I'm worried about her being stuffed in your backpack. Let's think of another way to get her safely to and from school." Laura offered Kim choices:

"Would you like to carry her in a box or in this shopping bag?"

"When you get to school, where can you put her so she'll be safe until it's time for show and tell? On the teacher's desk or in your cubby?"

"Are you going to pass her around the room so all your friends can see her up close and touch her, or are you going to hold her up yourself in front of the room protecting her?"

Any of the options were acceptable, but as Kim made each choice, it helped her feel in control of the situation and responsible for her doll as well.

By asking these questions, Laura helped Kim plan for and successfully manage the doll's trip to school. If the doll did get damaged, she would still know she did her best to set the stage for success.

Laura reviewed Kim's plan with her, "Okay, Kim,

you're ready to take your doll to school, she's safely in the shopping bag. Your plan is to put her in your cubby when you get to school. You've decided not to pass her around the room; you will hold her and walk her around the room for everyone to see. This is a great plan."

Then she cautioned, "Kim, please realize, something could still go wrong. Bullies could sneak her out of the bag and toss her around the room. You could drop the bag in a mud puddle by accident. I hope these things won't happen, because we'd both be very sad. Now, be on your way—have a good day."

Laura felt much better. She helped Kim develop a plan for success, but it was one where Kim held the controls. She didn't try to control the situation by forbidding Kim to take the doll to school, but she didn't just throw up her hands and let Kim take the doll off to school unprotected either.

You can't always safeguard your children against the frustrations and minor miseries life offers, but you can help them down the road to competency by thoughtfully offering choices which put them in charge of the situation and help them to plan ahead.

Incentives Provide Choice

Another option for ending a power struggle is to offer a choice using an incentive. As you now know, power struggles can quickly become embedded in a routine, a part of the parent-child relationship. Offering a child the choice to either work for a reward or not puts the child in charge of the situation. You hope that, in the process of working for a reward, your child will learn a new habit and thereby change his behavior, which in turn, will end the daily power struggle. The incentive program depersonalizes the situation. It is no longer a problem between parent and child—the focus moves to the child and his power to choose. He can work to acquire the prize or not.

An incentive program is used only for a limited amount of time. Once the new habit is acquired, then the parent phases out the reward system. Success is more likely if parents tackle only one behavior issue at a time. A reward system adapts to many situations and it's important not to overuse it. Too many charts for rewards tied to improved behavior can lead to confusion and frustration for both parent and child.

Another essential requirement for success is a matter-of-fact demeanor on the part of the parent. Offering the child a friendly reminder regarding the choices involved is okay, but any emotional response from a parent can reinforce the negative behavior. You need to gain control of your emotions before your child can improve his behavior. Save the passion in parenting for your child's positive behavior.

The Saturday Chores Power Struggle

 At Saturday morning chore time, Kevin, age eight, dragged his feet, complained and took hours to empty the garbage can in his bedroom, strip his bed sheets, and vacuum his bedroom. Mom prodded him along at first, then yelled for him to "Just get the job done!" Mom tried to convince Kevin that if he'd just forge ahead through his chores without all the complaining, he'd be off to play much sooner, but inevitably, she ended up finishing Kevin's chores herself. Mom wanted to change this negative routine. She knew Kevin was perfectly capable of performing these chores, yet refused, so she decided to try something different.

Resolution of the Saturday Chores Power Struggle

One day an opportunity presented itself. Kevin asked Mom for a Lego® space ship. Kevin knew it was expensive, yet he was yearning for the challenge of putting it together. Mom struck a bargain, "I know you really want that Lego® ship. I want something too. I really want you to finish your chores by noon each Saturday morning. When you do so without complaining, you'll receive one sticker. Six stickers will earn you the Lego® ship."

Mom was gambling that as Kevin worked for the space ship, he would acquire the habit of doing his chores quickly and then realize that chores really weren't such a burden after all.

But, you ask, shouldn't kids do chores without rewards? Certainly. Unfortunately, for some reason Kevin and his mom had fallen into this negative Saturday morning habit and power struggle. The situation needed to change, and the incentive system was a good way to accomplish this. Kevin had a choice. He could choose to do his chores by noon and eventually receive his Lego® set, or he could choose to drag his feet and delay or deny himself the toy he wanted. It was up to him whether or not he acquired the new Lego® set. Mom was out of the loop.

If Mom found herself becoming emotional again, it would be better to drop the incentive program altogether. There are many disciplinary techniques available to resolve power struggles, but none will work as long as the parent is emotional and out of control.

Each Saturday morning, Kevin's mom proceeded in the following manner:

Mom: "Kevin, I am reminding you to do your chores before noon this morning."

Kevin:"Okay, okay. I know."

Mom: "Just remember our bargain. Your chores need to be done by 12:00 o'clock. If not, no sticker for the Lego® set."

That's all she said until noon. If Kevin completed his work, she simply said, "You did your three tasks, good for you. Here's your sticker for the chart." If the jobs weren't done by noon, Mom simply stated the obvious, "It's 12:00 o'clock. Your chores aren't done, so no sticker this week.

You can try again next week for a sticker toward your Lego® set." If Kevin pleaded and cried, Mom would empathize, "I know you're disappointed you didn't earn your sticker. You can try again next week." She would say no more and get on with her day, completing the chores quickly herself.

Why should Mom complete the chores herself? Remember, her goal was to get her son to complete his chores each Saturday morning in a timely fashion. Rather than trying to overpower him, which was getting her nowhere, she presented him with a choice to complete his chores, receive a sticker, and eventually win the prize he was working toward, or to not finish chores in the designated time frame, not receive the sticker, and thus delay further acquiring the Lego® ship.

So if he chooses not to complete his chores, and Mom still needs those chores done, then she needs to do them. That's the deal. When offering choices, you need to be prepared for your child to choose either option.

It wouldn't be fair to give Kevin an additional consequence by taking away television or keep him from playing outside, since that was not part of the original deal. The agreed-upon consequence for Kevin is the delay in receiving the ship he's longing to put together. Whether the incentive program is a success depends on Mom's matter-of-fact attitude, and on Kevin's interest in winning the prize. He may keep choosing the negative path, not doing chores, not receiving the ship. If so, Mom will need to come up with another route to reach her goal.

Rules Provide Opportunities for Choices

Establishing a rule and a consequence is another method for ending power struggles. When making a rule, it's important for you to explain why you're making it and how you'll enforce it with a consequence. An established rule provides your child with a choice: one offers a positive consequence, the other a negative consequence. For example, if your child follows the rule, she continues on with her chosen activity. If she breaks the rule, you step in and impose an unattractive alternative. The choice is up to her.

You need to stay in close proximity to your child in order to restate the rule and remind her of the choices available. Usually it only takes about three days for the new behavior to become a habit, as long as you are calm and consistently enforce the rule.

Remember, when you offer a choice, you must be willing to live with whatever your child chooses. If he chooses the unattractive negative consequence, it's important to accept it. Kids are compelled to test new rules. Go ahead and let them. They usually come around to your way of thinking when they realize they're not going to get your dander up.

The School Gear Power Struggle

At the Runquist household, Dad wished he had trained his boys, ages five, seven, and nine, to put their school items away when each started kindergarten, but he had not. He has been angry many afternoons as he watched his boys bound through the door after school, dropping their coats, back packs, and lunch boxes in the hall as they headed first for the refrigerator and then the television.

From his arm chair, Dad yelled for them to put their things away, even sometimes calling the boys inconsiderate slobs. The boys ignored him. Later, Dad angrily would put all the items away himself. This episode set a tense tone for the entire evening.

This was another habitual power struggle. The boys didn't put their school stuff away because not doing so was part of their coming-home routine. Dad thought the boys would break this habit simply because he yelled at them to do so. Unfortunately, Dad didn't realize the boys unconsciously considered his yelling and angry stance a normal, predictable part of the afternoon routine.

Resolution of the School Gear Power Struggle

Dad established a new rule with a built-in consequence. When the three boys come home from after-school care, the TV stays off and the refrigerator does not open until the boys hang up their coats and back packs on the designated hooks in the family room and place their lunch boxes on the kitchen counter.

Now with a new rule in place, the boys have a choice; they can choose to put their things away and have a snack and watch a little TV, or they can choose to leave their items on the floor and skip the snack and TV. Dad imposed this rule and explained his reasons:

▶ Back packs, lunch boxes, and coats are the boys' responsibility, not his;
▶ Putting items away contributes to the overall functioning and organization of the household;
▶ When it's time for homework in the evening and school in the morning, the boys will be able to locate their belongings more easily when they're put away properly.

Dad's demeanor became composed when he greeted the boys at the door each afternoon and reminded them of the new rule and the choice each must make. After only three days, two of the boys quickly put their belongings in their proper places and then headed directly for the refrigerator and TV. This change of behavior happened quickly because Dad got out of his armchair and met his sons at the door and reminded them of the rule. The reminder and Dad's physical presence at the door helped change the afternoon routine and made the positive choice Dad hoped for.

Jason, the oldest, was angry about the rule and decided to make an issue of it. He dropped his things at the door and headed for his bedroom. Dad accepted his choice (remember, when you offer a choice, you must be willing to live with either outcome). As it turned out, Jason only chose the undesirable option for a few days; soon, he was complying with the new rule along with his brothers.

Compromising Through Formal Negotiation

Some power struggles can be resolved through negotiation. All family members involved in the problem participate in the negotiation process. Either a parent or child can open up negotiations. The first step is to clearly identify the existing problem. Here is how to do it:

Identify the problem. Although everyone in the family realizes a problem exists, each may see it differently. Before attempting to solve the problem it is important for everyone to discuss and identify as clearly as possible just exactly how they each view the difficult situation.

Take notes. It works best if a neutral family member actually takes notes. People often forget the details of an agreement, so when someone writes down ideas and decisions, the written agreement is available to refresh everyone's memory.

Brainstorm ideas. The rule of brainstorming is that nobody is allowed to criticize or put down anyone else's idea, no matter how outrageous. Everybody is encouraged to come up with as many creative solutions to the problem as possible. The note taker jots down all ideas.

Review the ideas. Once all the ideas are written down, participants review them, trying to find one or more solutions to the problem. The final solution must be acceptable to everyone. If one person involved cannot accept a solution, it is discarded.

Decide on the idea you all wish to try. Unanimous agreement is essential. If a solution cannot be agreed upon by all parties, table the problem until the next day. This gives everyone the opportunity to reevaluate the options. Once a solution is agreed upon, the note-taker writes down the solution so all can refer to it later. The parties involved sign it. It is the parent's responsibility to see the solution is carried out.

The Wall Poster Power Struggle

Ten-year-old Jerry made this simple request, "Can I put some posters up in my room?" Mom met this request with a flat out, "No, we just painted your room. Besides, I hate posters. They rip, they look terrible and when you take them down, the tape peels the paint." Jerry, a fairly compliant child, accepted Mom's refusal with disappointment, but without a battle.

Jerry was ready to take over more control of his life. Decorating and managing his bedroom was perfectly appropriate. But Mom turned him down cold.

This mom packed a powerful presence, she was in charge of the family and everyone knew it. She was a firm and confident parent, and most of the time, that worked well. But in this instance, when Jerry made a reasonable request to take some control over his bedroom, she presented the same rigid stance.

She didn't see Jerry's request as part of the natural process toward growth and autonomy, she was simply operating on automatic, proceeding in the same parenting mode as always. She didn't consider Jerry's request from his point of view.

What followed? Jerry turned sullen and surly. Where once he was agreeable, he turned argumentative. When asked by Mom to empty the garbage, he would say, "I'm not doing it and you can't make me." Then he'd take off on his bicycle.

Mom was puzzled. This was the first time Jerry had ever acted this way. Why now? What was going on? This situation between Jerry and his mom wasn't a full-blown emotional battle, it was another form of power struggle: when a child doesn't receive power and control in positive ways, he will seek it in negative ways. Mom refused Jerry the positive control he requested, so he received the control he was seeking by refusing to comply with her reasonable requests around the house.

Jerry's newfound belligerence wasn't coming from a conscious level. He didn't think, "Mom didn't give me what I wanted, so now I won't do as she says." That's not the way the push for self-governance works. When a child's time line for more control and independence conflicts with the parent's ability to let go of parental controls, misbehavior on the part of the child often results.

Resolution of the Wall Poster Power Struggle

So what's a parent to do? In this case, negotiate. The first step was to clearly identify the existing problem: Jerry wanted posters; Mom didn't want to bother with his request, but she did want his behavior to improve. Only Jerry and his mom were involved in the negotiations. Mom called a meeting. She and Jerry sat down to work out a compromise. Dad was the note taker.

Jerry and Mom's brainstorming ideas:

- ▶ No posters at all
- ▶ One poster on the wall
- ▶ Posters covering the entire wall like wallpaper
- ▶ A few posters put up with special tape that won't damage paint
- ▶ Mom putting up and taking down the posters
- ▶ Jerry deciding where and how many posters for his room
- ▶ Sports posters only; no music-related posters

The two reviewed the list and discarded the suggestions unacceptable to either Mom or Jerry. They agreed that Jerry would be allowed to tape a few baseball posters to the walls with a special tape, but Mom would be the one to remove the posters carefully.

This agreement was fairly easy to reach. Mom and Jerry signed a contract to formalize the agreement.

Parents compromise daily with their children, not only to avoid or resolve power struggles, but to build competency and independence in their children and to show children their needs are recognized and valued. It's probably the best and easiest way to solve family conflicts. Through negotiation, you can hold on to some of your power and control when necessary, while appropriately releasing some of it to your children.

In the negotiation process, there are no absolute winners or losers; everyone wins something and loses something. Usually the child is motivated to carry out the solution since he participated in the problem-solving process.

This technique develops creative thinking skills in children and it teaches them valuable social skills for interpersonal relationships. The use of this technique usually reduces hostility on the part of the child.

When Nothing Seems to Work

When you are working to end a power struggle, you may first, quite reasonably, work in the direction of offering choices, negotiating, or compromising on-the-fly. You may attempt to offer your child a series of choices that lead to competency. You might also try an incentive plan or offer choices—one leading to a positive consequence, the other a negative. If all these approaches fail, you may enter into formal negotiations leading to a compromise with your child. You may be perfectly matter-of-fact and calm in your demeanor and tone of voice as you communicate your plan to your child. You may have the best parenting intentions in mind, but nevertheless, your child balks, and still doesn't comply. Perhaps your child resists all your attempts as you work to reach the desired goal you've set, whether it's doing his homework, cleaning his bedroom, or something else which seems perfectly reasonable for his age and development.

Rather than a full-blown power struggle, this situation is more like a parent-child tug-of-war. Your child wonders what you'll try next, resists, may feel your attempts are manipulative, and even sabotages your plan. It becomes a game; the parent tries restricting the child and the child doesn't seem to care. The parent withdraws privileges and the child is unmotivated and disagreeable. Why? The problem may simply be that you have not laid the necessary groundwork and shaped the child's behavior (see Chapter 7) to accomplish the task successfully. Or the situation could be as complex as low motivation and interest to comply due to low self-esteem, childhood stress, even depression.

When you bump up against a brick wall in parenting, you may need to back off, re-shape, or teach remedial skills for homework or bedroom management or chores. In more worrisome situations, you may need to seek help from a family counselor, child psychologist, or when it comes to resistance to completing school work, talk to the teacher and possibly hire a tutor.

In such situations, parents sometimes must adjust their goals and change their parenting agenda. This path may be difficult for you to accept and carry out, but necessary for the long-term behavioral health of your child, as well as the parent-child relationship.

Now you know how to resolve power struggles by negotiation, compromise, and choices, which is where you'll invest most of your parenting time when you come up against your child's natural push for power and control. Next is the last option to resolving a power struggle, letting go or dropping out.

6

Letting Go of a Power Struggle

Letting go, dropping back or out, is the last option for resolving a power struggle with a child. If you're in a nightly battle about cleaning up toys, you might want to let go for a while, have a calming-down and cooling-off period, then later, try another approach for putting toys away. You're not dropping out completely, you're simply dropping back. You take the opportunity to collect yourself, work on the relationship with your child, and then later, try to exert your influence using a new approach.

How to Drop Out

If you have come to realize the demands you're making on your child are out-of-line for your child's developmental level, then dropping out is an appropriate option. For example, let's say you expected your two-year-old to dine in a restaurant. After many embarrassing restaurant scenes, you decided your expectations were unrealistic. So you dropped out of the battle by going only to fast food restaurants, bringing restaurant food home, or getting a sitter when you went to a restaurant that wasn't suited to two-year-olds. Later, when your child is more mature, you'll try taking her to a restaurant again.

When you set rules or standards for behavior, it's important, of course, to be consistent. But if you find yourself in an emotional battle of wills with your child as you attempt to establish the rule, the power struggle will actually keep your child from learning it. Power struggles get in the way of teaching skills, or establishing effective discipline. When this happens, drop out, relinquish the controls, take a rest, then develop a new approach later. It's a rest period that usually involves a change of tactics. Then when you develop a new approach, do so without arguing or escalating your emotional state.

When you do let go, do it with dignity. Don't throw up your hands and scream hysterically, "Just leave the toys all over the floor. We'll just live in this mess without any respect for our property. I'll clean it up, I always do anyway. Get out of here."

Instead, adopt a dignified demeanor, "You know, cleaning up toys has become a real hassle. I'm tired of arguing with you about it. You are more important to me than cleaning up these toys. I'll do it for now."

The paradox of dropping out of power struggles is that, when you do, your children usually come around to your way of thinking or behaving, and open up to your influence. The child who fought with you about tidying toys miraculously now volunteers to help.

When you let go and allow your child to grasp reasonable control of her life in an area that's of particular importance to her, or in an area like toileting where the child ultimately holds the controls anyway, the power struggle ends and the parent-child relationship is restored.

Dropping Out Is Not Giving Up

Clearly, it's not appropriate to continually drop out of power struggles. If you tend to do this a lot, that's permissive parenting. It will not produce responsible, well-disciplined children. You need to have the interest and energy to calmly and clearly hold on to a decision when it comes to your child's health, safety, or your family's values. Children need to understand that, in many situations, you'll be willing to negotiate, offer choices, and compromise. They also need to experience you holding on when appropriate, and dropping out when appropriate.

The occasional decision to let go gives you a chance to preserve and build your relationship with your child. Often when you drop back, you have the opportunity to look at your child with new eyes and gain a new perspective on the problem. You can learn how to better manage his behavior and develop an appreciation for his unique personality.

It's difficult for any parent to drop out of a power struggle because, when you do, you may feel you're losing a part of your parenting self, giving in, giving up. Sometimes it is necessary and represents quality parenting to relinquish control in order for a child to learn a skill or behavior, or manage herself without your interference. Although sometimes difficult to see or admit, by dropping out, you're giving your child the opportunity to succeed in her own right. It's hard to set aside the fear that your child will fail once out from under your control. Some parents even fear they won't be needed once their child develops her own competencies.

Projecting Ahead: Borrowing Trouble

Parental fear is a significant factor in power struggles. Six-year-old Matt's hair style was a battleground between him and his mom, June, because she projected ahead to the day when he might go to a job interview as an adult with an outrageous hair style. This tendency to project fearfully into the future blocks a parent's ability to manage the present situation thoughtfully.

June, who was locked in a power struggle, couldn't see that Matt's unusual choice today would probably satisfy his need for unusual hair styles, and he would most likely choose a more reasonable one the next haircut around.

Although this projecting ahead is common, and sometimes offers a broader, long-term perspective, it often keeps parents from effectively dealing with the situation at hand. June would even say, "I can't believe you're wearing your hair like that. When you go for a job interview in ten years, will you go looking like that?" Of course, Matt has no such thoughts, he is just thinking about today.

The Piano Practice Power Struggle

Carolyn was in a piano-practice power struggle with her eight-year-old son Chris. She feared her talented son would not reach his piano playing potential if he didn't practice, or worse yet, the reluctance to practice would spill over into all areas of his life. She worried he wouldn't work diligently at *any* endeavor.

With Chris's reluctance to practice the piano, Carolyn would say things like this, "You're supposed to be practicing! Are you going to be an irresponsible slacker your whole life?" Of course not, either Chris hadn't integrated practice into his daily routine, or maybe he was frustrated and avoiding the effort it takes to succeed. Maybe he lacked interest or talent, but his approach to the piano was unlikely to dominate all the tasks he would encounter in life unless his mother's prediction became a self-fulfilling prophesy and Chris took on the label, actually developing a slacker's approach to his life.

When Chris was finally at the piano, his mother corrected his playing skills. Her criticisms of technique and comments about misplayed notes and inconsistent rhythms added to his reluctance to practice and actually took away his desire to succeed.

The Mini-Mart Power Struggle

Evelyn and her nine-year-old son, Jeff, were locked in a power struggle. It played itself out each summer morning. Jeff wanted to walk about three-quarters of a mile to the neighborhood mini-mart for candy. Evelyn refused to let Jeff walk this distance. It wasn't unsafe; she had walked it many times with Jeff and knew he was cautious. Besides, there were no busy streets to cross. Jeff had walked similar distances to friends' houses, but Evelyn wouldn't allow the trek to the mini-mart. Why?

Evelyn explained, "I just don't like to see young kids milling around mini-marts without their parents. They don't go in and just buy their candy, they play video games and hang out with friends. They may steal something and then those same kids may end up smoking behind the mini-mart. No way will I let Jeff do it." She was projecting fearfully ahead to the future without any real basis in Jeff's behavior for her fear.

Jeff was relentless in his determination to travel to the mini-mart. He started begging at breakfast. Evelyn was calm at first, as she tried to explain her point of view. When Jeff's pleading continued, she'd escalate and explode. Then Jeff stomped off to his bedroom or outside to play. The mini-mart argument got the day started off on a tense note. Not only that, the power struggle was coloring Evelyn and Jeff's entire relationship. Jeff was surly and disrespectful. There were moments when Evelyn didn't even think she liked her son. Repetitive power struggles have a way of destroying parent-child relationships.

It's important to understand, Jeff was a nice kid, he was not a trouble maker. He didn't have any intentions of loitering, stealing, or smoking. He wasn't interested in playing video games or hanging out with friends. The mini-mart was just an adventure he wanted to try and he felt he was old enough and capable enough to meet this challenge.

Evelyn was fearful of what might happen as her son moved away from the nest and met the trials and temptations of the bigger world. Her fears clouded her ability to think clearly. She projected ahead and assumed Jeff would be lured into negative activities.

Of course, the situation Evelyn feared could actually happen, but children need to be given the chance to prove themselves as responsible as they push their boundaries at each developmental stage. If Jeff were attracted to a negative peer group at the mini-mart, then he would lose the privilege of going there. Right now, Evelyn might reconsider allowing him the opportunity to prove himself, especially since it's not an issue of safety.

Safety Concerns

Power struggles often do involve a child's safety. In past generations, children were allowed to travel on their bikes, go to the park, and build camps in the woods by themselves. With a "Be home by dinner time" reminder, children would go off for the afternoon with friends. Children would feel very competent as they rode off on their bikes with their pals, exploring and testing their competency in the big world.

Today, with the level of violent crime against children in some neighborhoods, such adventures are usually unthinkable. Responsible parents can't allow their children to go to the park without an adult until they're at least 10 years old, and even then only with two friends along. Parents must designate a house near the park where a friendly family lives for their kids to run to if there's trouble, and children can't be gone long. You must lay a safety net for your children as they venture out in the world beyond your immediate protection.

Although society has changed and parents' need to protect children has increased, children still have the same developmental push for adventure. Parents must put more effort into ensuring their children have safe adventures available to them. Allowing children to extend their physical boundaries is a common source of power struggles.

Resolution of the Mini-Mart Power Struggle

After consulting with friends and neighbors, Evelyn finally decided to relinquish control. She said, "Jeff, I've changed my mind and reconsidered you going to the mini-mart to buy candy. You have one dollar, I don't want you to spend more than that. Which pocket are you going to keep your money in? It's best if you go with one of your friends. Do you want to ask Jeremy or Kevin? You can be gone for thirty minutes, that's all. Do you have your watch on?"

Jeff and his friend didn't loiter, steal, or smoke at the mini-mart. They came home with candy and big smiles from having managed this adventure successfully.

Did Evelyn give in? Yes. Did she lose her authority and dignity in Jeff's eyes? No. Evelyn reconsidered the situation and dropped out with dignity. It's okay to change your mind. All parents wish they could use perfect judgment when it comes to managing children, but because you can't be experienced in everything, and every child is different, sooner or later, you will probably find yourself in this kind of power struggle. When you do, don't feel like you must hold on no matter what. You can drop out gracefully.

Resolution of the Hair Style Power Struggle

Letting go of the hair style power struggle ended this way for Matt and his mom. One day, at the salon where his mom got her hair styled, Matt picked out a style he liked for himself from one of the hair-styling books.

His mom's response was, "No way! You're not wearing your hair like that." Matt left the salon that day in tears. At home, he persisted in pleading for the "weird style," as his mom described it.

Every day Matt would comb his hair differently, trying to replicate the style of the man in the magazine. On the day when June was about to take him to the barber shop, Matt stomped his foot and yelled, "I'm not going! I hate the way the barber cuts my hair." Finally June acquiesced and scheduled an appointment at the design salon. The power struggle was over. She hoped that over the years his interest in wearing "weird" hair styles would diminish.

Resolution of the Piano Practice Power Struggle

This power struggle came to a head one day when Chris slammed down the cover on the piano keys yelling, "If you know so much about the piano, why don't you take lessons yourself?" Carolyn gulped. From that day on, she changed her tactics by dropping back. She said to Chris, "Your teacher expects you to practice 40 minutes every day, and it's my responsibility to see you follow through. You tell me the time each day when you plan to practice and I'll remind you. No TV, no other activity until your practice is done." Even though Chris complained and pouted his way to the piano, Carolyn insisted he practice every day.

Once he was at the piano, Mom set into motion her new approach. When Chris sat down to play, she only offered positive comments: "That's one of my favorite songs, will you play it again?" "Your practice time is my favorite time of day. The dishes go so much quicker with your music in the background. Thank you for playing." But what seemed to mean the most to Chris was when Mom would bring her needlework or a book into the living room, sit, and just listen. Chris's piano playing quickly improved and the power play was over. Piano was now a vehicle to build their relationship rather than a time to tear it apart.

With this supportive approach, the atmosphere in the house changed concerning piano playing. Most importantly, Mom could see her son really did have the ability to concentrate and work diligently.

Why Can't Children Just Comply?

Why does parenting have to be so difficult and complicated? Why can't children just do as they're asked and respect parents at the same time? Don't you wish kids would be compliant until they're eighteen, and then move out of the house as full-functioning, competent adults?

By now you know the answer. Children are born with the drive to be under their own control and to develop their own competencies. They need parents to guide them and then gradually back off as they learn to manage themselves. Although you may fantasize about having a compliant child, realize that compliant children often grow into compliant adults who return to their parents to make decisions for them. They've always done as they were told, had no practice making their own decisions, and continue their childhood dependency into adulthood. If they don't continue to depend on their parents, they often find a friend or mate who steps in and takes over where their parents left off.

Although you'll probably never welcome a power struggle, recognize it's happening because your child is fiercely independent and determined to develop her own abilities. She is practicing for the time when she's an adult and independent from you. The goal in parenting is not to have obedient children who are easily controlled, but children who will eventually operate autonomously. Children who are naturally submissive need encouragement from parents to gradually handle themselves.

Letting go isn't giving up, it's taking an alternative route that leads to your goal. Letting go requires you to adjust your frame of mind and relax, realizing that when you do, your child is often more easily influenced by your wishes.

You also need to let your child know that although piano practice and hair are important, neither is an issue of love. If your child wore a wild hair style every day of his life, would your love for that child end? If your child refused to practice the piano at all, would you withdraw your love? Of course not, but sometimes parents get so involved in power plays that a child might start to believe that a parent doesn't love him any more, that piano or hair is more important than the child himself. All you need to say is this, "You could wear that hair style till you're 65 and I would love you just the same. But for Grandma's birthday party, I would really appreciate it if you'd wear your hair a little less wild."

Now you're familiar with the three options for ending power struggles: hold on; offer choices, negotiate, and compromise; let go. In some routine battles, you can choose any one of the three viable options to end the power struggle. Just keep in mind, it's important to choose one and stick with it.

7

Choosing Any One of the Three Options

In some power struggles, it's perfectly clear which option to choose to end the battle, but in others, any one of the three options would work. The key is to pick just one and stick with it. Don't confuse your child by switching approaches midstream.

The Bedtime Power Struggle

Carrie developed a positive bedtime routine for Amber from the time she was 18 months old. Carrie would put Amber in her pajamas, brush her teeth, then read her a story. Next, Amber would request a drink of water. The bedtime routine ended with Mom offering Amber a kiss and a hug and tucking Amber's stuffed toy turtle in bed next to her. When Amber slept in a crib, she fell quickly to sleep.

When Carrie moved her to a single bed, Amber had freedom to roam. Carrie thought a simple command, "Now don't climb out of bed, it's time to go to sleep" would do the trick. Instead, it soon became the line that triggered the negative portion of the bedtime routine.

Once Amber was tucked into her bed, Carrie headed downstairs to relax after a busy day of working and parenting. As Carrie settled into the sofa each evening, she'd be a tad tense wondering if Amber would fall asleep without several trips downstairs and a tearful scene.

As Carrie turned on the television, she heard Amber quietly pad down the stairs. Sighing in exasperation, Carrie yelled, "Amber, go back up to bed right now." Quickly, Amber turned and headed toward her bedroom. Then she stopped at the top of the stairs, waited about thirty seconds, and then headed down the stairs again. Carrie chased Amber to her room, forcefully put her back in bed, pointed her finger at Amber and yelled, "Don't you dare get out of bed again!"

Despite the warning, three minutes later Amber made another trip down the stairs. This time Carrie chased her up to bed, slammed her bedroom door and held it shut as Amber cried herself to sleep. So ended the no-longer peaceful bedtime routine.

All parents know the importance of routine in the life of children. Routines make life predictable, and when positive, can make the transitions in the lives of busy parents flow smoothly. The routine Carrie established for Amber's bedtime started out positive and pleasant, but ended with screaming, yelling, and tears, until Amber would finally fall asleep.

It's important to realize that the negative portion of the bedtime routine is as embedded in the routine as the positive. It's not that Amber liked being yelled at and crying herself to sleep, it's just that it was part of the routine that played itself out every night before she would fall asleep; it made her life predictable.

Carrie wanted to end the routine, but how? What would work best in her present circumstance as a working, single parent? Each of the three options for ending power struggles had merit.

Options for Ending the Bedtime Power Struggle

1. Hold on to power and control. For this option, after the bedtime story, kiss, and hug, Carrie would need to park herself on a chair outside Amber's door and read the newspaper until Amber fell asleep. If she heard Amber get up, Carrie could quietly get up from her chair and state calmly and clearly, without any eye contact, "It's time to go to sleep, goodnight" and put Amber back to bed. If Amber persisted in getting out of bed, Carrie would close the door and repeat at five-minute intervals the same line, "It's time to go to sleep, goodnight."

Bedtime tears are difficult for some parents to bear. If Carrie chose the hard line method, it would be important for her to tell herself that Amber wasn't crying because she was lonely and desperate for her mommy; Carrie would be right outside her door. It would be the change in the bedtime routine Amber would be protesting. With this approach, Carrie would be giving Amber the opportunity to put herself to sleep without several trips in and out of bed and up and down the stairs. When parents attempt to change a negative routine into a positive one, the child's behavior often gets worse before it gets better, as the child tries to pull the parent back into the old pattern of behavior.

If Carrie chose this approach, it would take about three days for Amber to fall asleep without getting out of her bed. Amber would eventually feel secure with the new routine and also competent because she could put herself to sleep without a struggle. Then Carrie could move right down to the sofa after the kiss and hug.

Even after the new routine is in place, Amber might test it a couple of times by getting out of bed and heading downstairs. Children are compelled to test any new rule parents establish, so Carrie must expect it and remain consistent by putting Amber back to bed and repeating the new nighttime refrain, "It's time to go to sleep, good-night" as she calmly tucks Amber in bed. She must be prepared to use the same calm approach each time Amber tests the rule.

If Carrie can't manage the self-discipline this approach takes, or can't handle listening to Amber's distress, she can try the next option.

2. Compromise, negotiate, offer choices. In this case, the compromise would involve Carrie developing a plan to gradually change the routine. After the kiss and hug, Carrie could lie down by Amber's side until she falls asleep. Then, after three or four days of lying down by her side, she could sit on a chair next to Amber's bed until she falls asleep. After three or four days of doing that, Carrie could move outside Amber's door until she falls asleep.

With each step in the process, it would be important to keep Amber informed as Carrie gradually withdraws her support: "Now I'll sit by you until you fall asleep" and "Now I'll be sitting in a chair outside the door. I'll be there until you're asleep." If Amber talks or tries to get up, Carrie would repeat the same boring line, "Mommy's right here; it's time to go to sleep."

If Carrie uses this approach consistently, the negative aspects of bedtime will quickly end, and eventually, a new positive routine will take its place.

The benefit of the gradual withdrawal is that Carrie puts Amber through less distress as she slowly withdraws her support. Yet she still has a plan for Amber to fall asleep independently, without the trips downstairs involved in the original negative nighttime routine. This plan will give Amber the opportunity to learn to put herself to sleep.

If Carrie does not have the discipline or energy to carry out this plan, she can choose the last option.

3. Let go, drop out, drop back. In this power struggle,

dropping out would mean Carrie will allow Amber to fall asleep on the sofa while Carrie reads the newspaper and watches television. Then, once asleep, Carrie would take Amber to her bed.

Resolution of the Bedtime Power Struggle

Carrie chose option number three. Why? Carrie works all day and Amber attends a child care home. Carrie is tired and stressed; she simply doesn't have the energy to tackle either of the other options. And besides, since Carrie and Amber aren't together all day, Carrie decides that she'd just as soon keep Amber close as she falls asleep and have a little time to relax herself. She doesn't want to put Amber or herself through a more complicated or stressful process to end the power struggle.

When Carrie chose the letting go option, the power struggle ended, no more trips down the stairs, no more tears and yelling. Carrie knew there would be a day when she'd want to put Amber to bed and have her stay there, but decided it would be easier when Amber turned three or four. Carrie might reconsider the first or second option then.

To some, this approach might seem like taking the easy way out, or that the child won. Considering the stress in Carrie's life, however, this was probably the best option. To tackle a more stressful solution would probably have ended in failure.

Also, it would be ill advised for Carrie to try one approach on one night and another a different night. Changing options would confuse Amber, leaving her wondering, yet interested, what approach Carrie would try next.

Most importantly, the power struggle was over for Carrie and Amber, both having got what they needed: Carrie had some time to relax and Amber had permission to fall asleep right by her mom's side.

Stressful Circumstances Require Letting Go

If your family is in a period of stress, and the power struggle you're involved in isn't an issue of safety, it's probably best to choose option three—letting go, dropping out or dropping back. If you have a new baby, if one of your parents is seriously ill, if there's been a death in your family, if you've just lost your job, if there's discord between you and your spouse, if your child is starting or changing schools or child care, or if you're moving, it's best to drop back until the stress passes.

When you're under stress, options one and two usually end up failing. The stress in your own life tends to keep you from concentrating, or maybe you just don't have the energy to succeed with the plan you're attempting. In addition, you typically have a hard time maintaining a calm demeanor when you're stressed. If your emotions are on a roller coaster ride, you will probably end up blowing your cool with your children.

If you choose to let go, don't feel defeated. It's a viable option. Remember, often when you drop out of a power struggle, the situation miraculously remedies itself. It's an option that sometimes takes care of the problem quite nicely.

Jumping Among the Three Options

As you now realize, the most confusing and least effective way to end a power struggle is to jump among the three options. This is what occurred in the power struggle situation at the Williams's house.

The Clean-Up Power Struggle

Five-year-old James dawdled when it was time to put his toys away. He took 15 minutes just to put his marking pens in the art box. Mom and

Dad Williams yelled at him, holding onto their power and control by refusing to let him eat dinner until all the toys were put away. James continued to poke through clean-up time, and dinner was delayed until finally Mom and Dad angrily threw the toys into their proper containers in the toy room.

On other evenings, Mom and Dad offered James a choice, but it operated more like a threat, "If you don't put your toys away, we're going to give them to children who will appreciate them. You have a choice, either clean up the toys or we're giving them all to the thrift store." James did nothing, and Mom and Dad eventually cleaned up the toys. They didn't follow through with their threat. Other times, Mom and Dad asked James to put his toys away, but he continued to sit and watch television. So, tense with exasperation, they hounded James about his irresponsibility and gave up their attempt to get him to put his toys away. With no consistent plan and the emotion-packed responses of his parents, James was resistant and confused. He did not become competent with regards to putting his toys away. Mom and Dad needed to develop a consistent plan and adopt a matter-of-fact attitude.

Resolution of the Clean-Up Power Struggle

James's parents chose option two, negotiate, compromise, or offer a choice. They combined it with a technique referred to as shaping. They realized making James tidy the entire room was overwhelming for him and left them all feeling frustrated. So they decided to gradually teach him how to clean up the room full of toys, step by step.

At 5 o'clock Mom and Dad set a timer and told James that he must put all his toy cars in the blue laundry basket within 15 minutes. They offered this warning, "The cars left on the floor after the buzzer sounds will go to the thrift store tomorrow."

Sounds harsh? Maybe. Mom and Dad could have

chosen to put the leftover cars in storage for a week, but they looked around James's playroom and saw far too many toys. They'd given him too much and decided that donating the toys would teach him to put them away when told. To learn to give unneeded items to others who have less was another family value they wished to instill.

The first night, James slowly put about half of the cars into the basket. Mom and Dad tidied the rest of the playroom. When the buzzer went off, Dad put the cars left on the floor in a bag for the thrift store. James cried and pleaded for a second chance, but Dad was firm, "No, these cars go to the thrift store tomorrow."

The following day, Mom and James took the cars to the thrift store after kindergarten. The next evening at 5 o'clock Mom asked James to put his cars in the blue laundry basket while she put the rest of the toys away. She set the timer for 15 minutes. Without hesitation, James completed the task. His parents praised him, "Look at that, you put all your cars in the basket. Good for you, we're proud of you. Now the room is neat and tidy and ready for play when you come home from school tomorrow."

Mom and Dad proceeded with the same plan for the next three evenings. On the fourth evening, they added a task to James's clean-up responsibilities: he now had to put the blocks in the red laundry basket, as well as put the cars in their designated basket. His parents continued to set the timer for 15 minutes.

For three weeks they proceeded in the same manner, adding a task and giving the most praise for the last responsibility added to James's list. At first, Mom and Dad helped James each evening. Later, they provided visual and verbal support, "I can't help you any more. Cleaning up the toys is your responsibility, but I'll watch you. Look, you finished your job in just 10 minutes! Way to go!"

If James wanted to leave a train track up for a couple

of days, his parents were not so rigid as to insist it be dismantled for the sake of total tidiness.

Within three weeks James was almost completely independent when it came to cleaning up his playroom. His parents did not need to use the thrift store threat again. James tested the rule once and learned immediately his parents meant business. Not only was the power struggle over, but James felt competent about his new skill for managing his play space.

This gradual teaching procedure, shaping, is useful for teaching a variety of skills, anything from teeth brushing, to getting dressed, to completing homework assignments. It's important when shaping your child's behavior to make certain it's a task your child is capable of learning. It's key to praise, call attention to, and show interest in the child's newly developed skill as she learns each step. Doing the task with your child is helpful, along with having clear rules for what you expect. Then you gradually withdraw your praise and the child's dependency on your presence.

Carrie and the Williams parents were in power struggles, not because Amber and James were pushing for more control in their young lives, but because their children were not adequately shaped, trained, or taught to perform the tasks their parents expected: Amber to fall asleep alone, James to tidy up after a day of play.

You may not be involved in a power struggle that involves bedtime or cleaning up toys, but whatever your negative power struggle routine, you might be able to end it by adapting the shaping procedure.

When you develop a plan, be sure to pick one of the three options. Jumping among the three options seldom ends a power struggle. Also, realize there are simply some power struggles you can't win, because your child, and your child alone, holds the controls.

8

Power Struggles You Will Always Lose

In parenting, it is important to identify what you can and can't control. You have tremendous influence in the life of your children—you can use that influence positively to guide their behavior. In a few areas, however, it's important to know specifically where your control begins and ends. Don't enter into power struggles over eating, sleeping, and toileting habits. Don't attempt to control your child's attitude, pace, internal thoughts, and emotional responses. Don't try to change your child's innate temperament.

Eating

You can encourage a child to eat by offering nutritious foods, limiting junk food, providing five small meals a day, and by making the meal-time atmosphere pleasant. You can even establish a rule requiring children to sit at the table for a reasonable amount of time for their age. But if a child flatly refuses to eat a food item, you can't force it down his throat. Only the child controls what he swallows.

One evening, two-year-old Alan refused to eat peas for dinner. His mom demanded, "Alan, you're going to sit in your high chair until you eat two peas." Janet started to clean up the dishes, then turned to see the peas on the high chair tray had disappeared. Did Alan eat those peas as his mom demanded? No, he stuck them up his nose. Who won this battle? Not Mom, that's for sure.

Sleeping

The same goes for sleeping. You can create a lovely bedtime routine for your child, easing him into bed after a story and prayer. You can sit outside your child's door so he can't escape his room, but if the child isn't sleepy, there's no way to demand he fall asleep. He, and he alone, holds the controls.

Toileting

Toileting is similar. When potty training your child, there is much you can do to encourage your child to use the toilet, but if your child digs in her heels and says, "No, I'm not going to poop in that toilet," it's best if you drop back for now and try to gently reassert your influence at another time. Bowel and bladder control lies with the child, not you. If you're already in a battle over toileting, go ahead and openly relinquish your attempts at control. Say, "I understand, you don't like pooping in the toilet. I'd like you to sit on the toilet and practice twice a day. If you go, that's fine. If not, that's fine too, it's your body. Someday you'll go in the toilet just like Mom and Dad, and your sister and brother, but when you do is completely up to you."

Relinquishing your attempts to control your child's bowel or bladder is often all it takes for the child to make progress. The child develops competency which she yearns to acquire, but in her own way and time.

Attitude

Wouldn't you like to control your child's attitude? Wouldn't you like your child to be cheerful about your request to set the table? Every parent would like her child to happily say, "Sure, Mom, I'll be glad to help." This is what all parents would like, but many children will complain as they go about a task. If your child is grumpy as she sets the table, let it be. You can't control your child's attitude, nor can you talk her into exhibiting a more pleasant one.

Saying, "Snap out of it. Make an attitude adjustment, will you?" is just a waste of time. Once you say this, the child will most likely exhibit that negative attitude all the more. For the child with a pouty, surly, or belligerent attitude, no amount of talk will convince her to let go of it.

Don't say this either, "If you're going to be such a grump about it, just forget about setting the table." If a grumpy attitude is all it takes to relieve the child of a chore, you'll see that attitude surface more and more, simply to escape the task.

You don't want the child's negative attitude to supply him with power. If a child gets a lot of attention for the negative attitude he's exuding, you'll see it more often. In addition, a negative attitude can become contagious, putting the entire household on edge.

The only attitude you can control is your own. You can see that your child's attitude doesn't affect yours, but if you're in a power struggle with your child about the importance of having a positive attitude, you'll lose. Here again, your child is in complete control.

Although you can't control your child's attitude or emotions, you can set reasonable limits on her behavior. For example, you can say something like this, "You're mad because it's your job to set the table. You can be mad, but the job is yours anyway. I'm leaving the room while you set the table because I don't like being here while you're stomping around."

Pace

Everyone moves at a different pace, and your child's pace may be different from yours. If you need to get out the door to work by 8 a.m., you'll be rushing around making sure you're on time. A young child doesn't understand work schedules. She might prefer to ease into the day by escaping into a world of imaginative play. If your pace and hers conflict, a dawdling power struggle may result.

If this power struggle happens in your home, realize that the burden of getting out the door in a timely fashion falls totally on you. Prepare for the morning ahead of time. Set out clothes and make lunches in the evening. Prompt your child through each step of the morning, "Do you want to put your shoes on, or do you want me to put them on for you?" Also give yourself enough time without calling too much attention to the fact that your child moves at a snail's pace.

If you are in a getting-out-the-door power struggle with an older child who fully understands work and school schedules, you must do some retraining. You'll need to go back to setting out clothes at night and prompting the child through each step of the morning, eliminating any negative aspects of the morning routine that focused on your child's slow pace. By doing so, you hope to end the existing, repetitive power struggle, and at the same time you'll learn to work with and understand your child who just naturally moves at a slower pace than you or a sibling.

Thinking

You cannot control your child's thinking. You can influence your children's values and opinions slowly, in a low-key yet determined way. But if you engage in a power struggle over your child's internal mental thoughts, you'll lose. Your child alone controls her thinking processes.

Three-year-old Abby misbehaved by coloring on the walls of her bedroom. Dad sent her to her room to "think about" what she did wrong. This consequence is silly when you consider it. Dad demanded that Abby spend a little time in her room, after all he was mad and he wanted her out of his sight for a minute or two, but could he really control what she was thinking about once in her room? It's likely his direction, "Think about what you did wrong" only fell on deaf ears. Abby knew it was wrong to color on her walls, but she just couldn't stop herself. The big bare wall looked to her like a big piece of paper. Off to her room Abby went, but she probably did not think about the importance of coloring on paper instead of bedroom walls. Having Abby wash the coloring marks off the walls would have been a more effective consequence.

Sean, eight years old, had a spelling test the next day. Instead of studying, he spent most of the evening logged onto the Internet, a favorite pastime. When Mom discovered this, she blew up, turned off the computer, and demanded Sean sit at the kitchen table and memorize his spelling words. Sean sat there and looked at his spelling words, but he didn't learn them, he was mad because Mom interrupted his session on the Internet. Mom could take him away from the computer and sit him in front of his spelling words, but she couldn't force him to learn to spell those words. Sean held the controls. Mom might have proceeded more effectively by saying this, "I know you have a spelling test tomorrow. I'll give you 15 more minutes on the Internet and then it's time to go over your spelling words. Let me know if you'd like me to quiz you."

You can talk to your child until you're blue in the face about the importance of keeping a tidy bedroom. Your argument may be reasonable, but nevertheless, if your child doesn't agree with the importance of keeping a tidy room, you're not going to convince him to think as you do. It's more effective to use teaching techniques instead. Try bringing your child into the room and pointing out specific areas to tidy. Offer several "how to" steps: "Put all your books on this shelf, then put your dirty clothes in the hamper. When you're done, we'll make your bed together—I'll show you how."

Emotions

In addition to being unable to control your child's thoughts, you can't control your child's emotional response to a particular situation either. You can put your child into a variety of situations, but how he responds emotionally is out of your control.

Shelly's three-year-old son, Zach, was excited to go to Grandma's birthday party, but he threw a temper tantrum when all the presents went to Grandma and not him. Shelly expected him to be happy for Grandma, after all, he turned three the week before and received plenty of gifts for himself. Shelly feared her son was becoming greedy as she watched him demand more presents.

In reality, Zach wasn't thinking about last week's gifts, he only wanted more when he saw Grandma's pile. Shelly couldn't talk her child out of his frustration and disappointment. What did she do? First of all, she didn't take the easy road and promise to buy him a present later. She simply picked him up, took him out of the room, and stayed with him until he was calm. She said, "I know you'd like a gift too. You wish all those presents were for you, but they're not. You can be angry, and I'm not going to let your tantrum ruin Grandma's birthday. When you're calm, we'll go back to the party."

Ken and his seven-year-old daughter, Chelsea, were flying home on an airplane after a five-day trip to Disneyland. Chelsea was pouting because she only rode on the Matterhorn Bobsled twice and wanted one more ride. Ken launched into a lecture about appreciating the trip rather than complaining. Chelsea continued to pout and found even more to complain about. The more Ken tried to convince her she should be happy about the trip, the more she was determined to prove the trip disappointed her.

If you try to talk your child out of her emotional response, you only prove to her that you haven't really heard what she had to say; in response to you, she will try to convince you further. Although it's difficult, when children respond to any situation emotionally, the best way to quiet those emotions is to put the child's feelings into words and just accept the emotional response. Ken might have said, "You really enjoyed the Matterhorn ride and you're disappointed you didn't get to ride on it one more time."

Don't allow any inappropriate behavior that accompanies the feeling, such as hitting or yelling. If the child is disturbing others, it's best to remove her from the scene. Stay with her to help absorb those out-of-control feelings, but don't try to talk her into feeling differently. Your child alone holds the controls. Feelings accepted, dissolve; feelings denied or suppressed, fester and then resurface at inappropriate times.

Temperament

Another area to think about when it comes to avoiding power struggles is your child's innate temperament. Everyone is born with nine temperamental characteristics. These nine inborn traits can even out as children develop, but if you take it upon yourself to change your child's innate personality, the likelihood is great you'll magnify, rather than diminish, those personality characteristics. Pushed to change, the persistent child becomes more persistent, the intense child more intense, the active child more active. You can't tell your child to be someone different than who she was born to be. Only through acceptance and working effectively with the child's personality can some of the more difficult temperamental characteristics smooth out.

Read through the following temperamental characteristics so you know not to engage in a power struggle with children regarding their innate personalities.

Persistence. Some children are just naturally more persistent than others. If you have a persistent child, you know how difficult he can be at times. But since persistence is a quality that can serve anyone well, you need to work with this characteristic, rather than try to make it go away.

On the other hand, if you have a child who doesn't persist at anything, never really gets into any project or activity, or seldom seems to follow an idea or interest with determination, this can also be frustrating. With this child, your job will be to help her learn to stay on task. Whatever degree of persistence your child has, it's part of who she is. Don't fight it; your pressure to change only accentuates that characteristic more.

Activity level. Some children simply come into the world more active than others. If you're active and energetic and give birth to a child who is happy to lie on the couch, you'll most likely do anything to get that child to do something physical. Do what you can, but don't engage in a power struggle over it.

Likewise, if you're a quiet person who likes to read, and your child is always on the go, running around, or squirming in a chair, you might have a difficult time adjusting to your child's activity level. Sometimes you'll want to scream, "Can't you just sit down and read a book?" If he could put it into words, your child might reply, "No, I'm active, don't try to change me. I'll read a book when I'm tired out, but for now, I've just got to run around the house and burn off some of the excess energy I was born with."

Approach and withdrawal in new situations. Some children enter new situations easily. Even as toddlers, you'll see them enter a family gathering with ease, toddling around comfortably, going from person to person. Others take longer to warm up to new situations. This doesn't mean they're shy or socially inept, it just means that, in a new situation, they need a little time by your side to become accustomed to the newness of it all. Some cultures admire people who are socially glib and jump right into social situations with ease and grace. Other cultures don't hold this trait so dear. They admire the person who holds back, assesses the situation, and then slowly enters. Either approach is okay.

You, as the parent of a child on either end of the approach and withdrawal continuum, need to simply accept your child's style. Just remember, the child who is slow-to-warm up is not necessarily shy, so don't saddle your child with that label. Some children just need to ease slowly into new situations and then they just might become the life of the party.

Adaptability to change. If you move households, introduce a new baby into your family, and buy a new car, all in the same month, one child might accept these changes without missing a beat, but another child might balk. Obviously, the child who adapts easily to change is easier to manage. The child who resists change needs time, reassurance, and nurturing through life's ups and downs. Starting school, going from a crib to a single bed, and going on vacation can cause sleepless nights and cranky days. Trying to talk this child into being more flexible is a waste of time. Learn to prepare this child for change; ease him into each situation and try not to allow too many changes at once.

Level of sensitivity. Some children are sensitive to light, temperature, noise, and stimulation in their environment; others never notice any of these. Children who are sensitive respond to stimulation by either winding up—being overly active—or by shutting down and fading into the woodwork. One mom whose child is easily stimulated deliberately arrives first to their parent-child class. The early arrival allows her child to gradually adjust to all the activity. If he starts running around from over-stimulation, the mom doesn't punish him; instead, she takes him out until he's calm and then they enter again. Punishing the child would only make this temperamental characteristic worse.

Regularity. Some children sleep, eat, and have a bowel movement at the same time each day. With others, you never know when any of these things will take place. Every day is different. Children with a natural schedule that more or less matches society's adjust easily to scheduling and particularly to the routines of family and school. But other children, who are irregular in their natural schedule, find it difficult to fit into such routines; they simply march to the beat of a different scheduling drum.

Don't engage in a power struggle with your child over following certain established norms. Instead, work to create positive routines and simple transitions from one activity to the next.

Distractibility. Some children are easily distracted, flitting from one activity to the next. They have trouble focusing on an activity, especially if there are many things going on around them. They simply notice and are interested in all that's going on. The distractible child has trouble concentrating on school work in a busy classroom. A child who gets intensely focused and has trouble leaving one task to go to another is also challenging. A child at either end of the spectrum can frustrate parents and teachers. Both must learn to accept and work with, not against this trait. Fighting against or calling too much attention to this temperamental characteristic only accentuates it.

Intensity. The intense child sobs loudly when sad and her temper tantrums last for a long time. When she's happy, she shrieks with enthusiasm. Demanding that this child mellow out is ridiculous; she feels every emotion intensely. These children are exciting individuals, but can wear out a parent or teacher in short order. The key is to help this child focus her intensity in positive ways; help her put that passionate energy into projects and activities where she can use the full force of her intense approach to life.

At the opposite end of the continuum is the mellow, laid-back child who never gets too excited about anything. If you're an intense parent, you might beg this child to show some exuberance for life. But realize, this child feels everything you do, just at a lower level of intensity.

Quality of mood. Some children are born seeing the cup half full, others see it half empty. Some children look on the positive side, others look at the negative. It's hard to believe children are born with this temperamental characteristic. If you're a positive person, you'll try to convince your child to look for the good in everything. But if you continually do this, your child will feel equally determined to convince you his perspective is valid—by telling you what went wrong at his birthday party, what he doesn't like about his bedroom, or what he can't stand about his teacher.

The positive child born to a negative parent can have the opposite effect. You might not appreciate your daughter's "Pollyanna-ish" approach to life. You want your child to have a more realistic approach. You can offer your opinion, but don't try to force agreement, it's a waste of time.

Understanding a child's innate temperament is complicated. For further information on this topic, refer to the suggested readings at the back of the book.

If you are in power struggles with your children over certain aspects of their lives, aspects that they absolutely control themselves, you'll only experience frustration and your relationship with your children will suffer. Drop out, relinquish your control, and develop a new, more realistic approach. In addition, it's important for you to look at yourself to see what you might be bringing to the struggle and why.

No-Win Situations
- Eating
- Sleeping
- Toileting
- Attitude
- Pace
- Thoughts
- Emotional response
- Temperament

9

What You Bring to Power Struggles

Some parents find themselves in power struggle after power struggle with their kids. Others don't get into a variety of struggles, but find themselves locked into the same power struggle day after day. If you are in such a situation, it's important to look inside yourself to see what responsibility you may have for the power struggle and why. Following are seven possible reasons parents often end up in power struggles. Inexperienced parents with unrealistic expectations is perhaps the most common.

Powerful Parents

Some parents with lots of power—the chairman of the board, the president of the PTA, the entrepreneur who runs her own business out of her house while managing her home and kids—think wrongly that if they have the skill to manage their professional lives in an effective (and often dictatorial) fashion, they should be able to manage their children in a similar way. One dad expressed his frustrations this way, "I operate my own business, am effective with clients and my employees. Yet once home, I can't get my three-year-old to clean up her toys. She can reduce me in minutes to a raving maniac. I just don't get it." Strategies you use with adults do not necessarily work with children.

Powerless Parents

Parents with little power find themselves in power struggles for a different reason. Janie stays home with her two little children. Her husband dominates her, telling her how to dress, run the house, and take care of the children. He doles out money, keeping tight control on what she spends at the grocery store and elsewhere. She has little control of her own life, so it becomes very important for her to control her children's behavior. She expects their rooms to be tidy, for them to remain perfectly dressed and spotless, and to clean their plates at every meal. Her day is filled with emotional battles as she tries to exert power over her children. Because she lacks appropriate power and control in her own life, she tries to make up for it by dominating her children.

Parents Who Seek the Ideal Child

Parents who think they can make their child fit a certain "ideal" mold find themselves in a long-term, continuous power struggle with that child. These parents picture in their minds an ideal child without considering the child's own uniqueness or individuality.

Melanie imagined raising a popular, active, smart, and feminine girl. When her daughter Stephanie started preschool, she played quietly, mostly with one other girl, never drew much attention to herself, and insisted on jeans instead of the dresses her mother wanted her to wear. By elementary school, she became bookish, never participated in sports or extra-curricular activities, sticking close to one particular friend. Mom pushed her into Scouts, maneuvered her onto a soccer team, and pleaded with her to wear more trendy, girlish clothes. She even coerced her into having skating parties by telling her that if she didn't have one, she couldn't play with her best friend after school for a week. She tried to fit her child into the profile of the ideal girl she envisioned.

Instead of appreciating the unique child she gave birth to, Melanie feared her daughter's personality reflected negatively on her; she neglected to keep her child's best interests in mind. She used her power inappropriately to direct her daughter's activities and interests.

Of course, parents must set standards for behavior and expectations for achievement, but when parents forcefully try to mold their child in such a way that conflicts with the child's innate temperament and personality, a unique type of power struggle develops.

Some children battle such parents; others, sadly, lose themselves trying to please the parent, but never quite managing to do so. These children become overly self-conscious, striving relentlessly for a parent's approval; others give up, accepting the fact that they'll never measure up, and stop trying to blossom into the person they were born to be.

Perfectionist Parents

Another circumstance that brings parent and child to the point of a struggle occurs when a parent is determined to have a child complete a task or act a certain way; there's only one way, the parent's way. These parents are often perfectionists, with a narrow margin of acceptance and little tolerance for behavior that deviates from their standards or point of view.

Some parents are perfectionists regarding their child's appearance. They pick out the child's clothes and blow dry her hair to perfection. If the child wants to wear a Mickey Mouse shirt that doesn't match his pants, the parent won't allow it and requires the child to wear a perfectly matching set of clothes. Perfectionists are determined to control certain aspects of their children's lives, sometimes at the price of the child's mental health.

Parents with Unrealistic Expectations

Other parents get into power struggles with their children because they have unrealistic expectations for their children's behavior or ability to achieve. Unrealistic expectations can result from unreasonable desire or from inexperience with children.

If you expect your three-year-old to get dressed all by herself without help or guidance, you may find yourself in a power struggle. The task is just too overwhelming for a child that age. She may start, but get distracted and appear to be dawdling while she is really engaged in fantasy play. Then she waits for the getting-dressed routine to end. How? With you yelling in exasperation and dressing the child yourself.

If you're trying to teach your child to dress herself, teach her in baby steps, stay right by her side, and give her specific directions, "Put your panties on. I'll watch you." You also need to notice and describe the child's actions that you want to reinforce, "I see you're putting your shirt on, good for you. Look at you, you're all dressed. What a kid!" As your child becomes competent, then gradually withdraw your presence.

It's not uncommon for parents to have unrealistic expectations. Why? It's usually because they lack knowledge of what children are appropriately capable of at different ages and stages, and sometimes it's just because they don't want to be bothered with the rigorous effort and patience it takes to guide a child to mastery of a skill.

Mike expects his five-year-old son to be up promptly at 7 o'clock in the morning, dressed, and eating breakfast by 7:30, then ready for child care and in the car by 7:45 a.m. He doesn't think his son needs time to ease into the day, reminders, or prompting. Mike considers him a little man and he should proceed as Dad does, without any morning lap time, play time, or attention from Dad. Consequently, mornings end up with Mike yelling and his son crying. Mike's inexperience and lack of understanding of his child's emotional needs keep the power struggle in place.

Parents Who Want Their Child to Complete What They Didn't

Sometimes parents want their children to complete something they themselves couldn't complete. There's the dad who wanted to play baseball when he was in high school, but couldn't because he had to work to help support his mom and siblings after their dad deserted them. With all the best intentions, he now pushes his son to play ball. Unfortunately for the father, no matter how he tries to influence his child toward an interest in athletics and especially baseball, the son prefers computers and chess; team sports leave him frustrated and overwhelmed. A power struggle between father and son occurs.

Parents Whose Children Must Succeed as They Did

Sometimes a parent wants his child to follow in his footsteps. He might think that what he did was the right thing, done in the right way, the only way, or the best way, so his child should do exactly the same. This parent doesn't take into consideration the personality, intelligence, and temperament of his child, or more importantly, the child's need to manage parts of his own life. This is what happened to Jim and his son Philip.

The Homework Power Struggle

Jim and his eight-year-old son, Philip, were locked in a power struggle that played itself out every day after school. Dad demanded, "You will do your homework right after school." Philip refused, "No, I won't and you can't make me. I'll do it when I want to."

Jim operated his business out of the family's house, so he was home each afternoon when Philip walked in the door. Dad insisted Philip do his assignments right after school. In second grade, when Philip first started bringing home assignments, Jim would sit with Philip and they would complete Philip's homework together.

Third grade started out the same way. Mom thought Dad was too involved in the way he took over. The homework was mostly Dad's effort, not Philip's. By the middle of third grade, Philip protested. He didn't want to do homework right after school. He wanted to play outside with a friend or watch television first. The argument started this way. Philip would say, "I can do it after dinner." Dad would respond, "No, you can't. We've always done it right after school. You've got to have your priorities straight. Now sit down at this table and get busy."

Philip would sit there but he'd dawdle, he'd slouch, he'd doodle on his paper, he'd act bored. This made Dad furious. Both father and son dug their heels in and the power struggle persisted every day until around 8 p.m. when Dad ended up completing 85% of Philip's homework.

Jim was extremely angry over the homework issue. When anger takes over, thinking stops. But the anger was only covering up Dad's fear. He was projecting ahead to Philip's high school years, seeing him refusing to do his assignments and then flunking classes, possibly dropping out of high school and never going to college.

Fear clouded Jim's thinking regarding Philip's approach and attitude toward homework. That fear prevented him from effectively dealing with the immediate situation. It's easy for us to see an obvious solution or compromise: why couldn't Philip decide for himself when to do his homework? After dinner would be fine. But Jim wouldn't consider letting Philip choose his homework time and place. He wanted his son to succeed the same way he did. Jim had been an excellent student himself; when he was in school he came home every afternoon, completed his assignments, and then took it easy the rest of the evening. You can't argue that this isn't an admirable approach, but it's unrealistic for Jim to expect Philip to accept the exact same homework routine.

So, what started as a simple disagreement about when Philip should do his homework became a full-blown power struggle. Philip wasn't completing his assignments, Dad was doing most of the work for him, and every afternoon and evening resulted in a heated battle between father and son, damaging their relationship.

Philip may have really wanted to do his homework but he didn't want to be controlled by Dad. He simply wanted to choose when and where to do it. He wanted to do it at the kitchen table without Dad constantly looking over his shoulder prompting him, and he wanted to do it after dinner. Dad's desire to control the situation prevented him from allowing Philip reasonable choices.

Dad had good intentions—he really believed he knew what was best for his son. Philip, on the other hand, did not want to be under his dad's control; he believed he could manage homework on his own.

Philip's grades were suffering as well as the father-son relationship. There was so much turmoil in the house each evening that all were desperate for the battle to end. Jim finally sought professional help.

Resolution of the Homework Power Struggle

Because the power struggle reached this magnitude, the only option for Dad was to drop out of the conflict. Early on in this power struggle scenario, Dad and Philip could have negotiated a compromise, but at this point, it was too late for compromise. Philip wanted to be left alone.

Although it was difficult for Jim to see at the time, by dropping out he was giving Philip the opportunity to succeed in his own right. It was hard for him to set aside the fear that Philip would fail once out from under his control. Jim even feared he wouldn't be needed any more once Philip developed his own competencies.

How did Jim drop out of the homework power struggle? He mustered up some courage, and with dignity made this statement, "Philip, I've reconsidered the homework situation and decided that it is your responsibility. If you need help I'm available. There will be no TV and no telephone calls on school nights after dinner. I hope you use this time to do homework, but if you don't, you will have to face the consequences with your teacher. I know you want to do well in school. It's up to you. I trust and expect that you will live up to your academic responsibilities." Jim let go of the homework power struggle and dropped out of the fight.

Then came a calming down and cooling off period in which Philip was to grasp hold of his homework responsibilities. He also tested his dad's promise to back off completely. It was painful for Jim to watch Philip waste time each evening. When Philip hurried through assignments in the morning at breakfast, it was hard for Dad not to say anything, but he didn't. He quietly left the room.

After about a month Philip started to do some of his homework after dinner. After about three months Dad was able to sit at the kitchen table, working on business matters, while Philip completed his assignments. He wouldn't help or interfere unless Philip asked, but he was there. His presence emphasized his support of Philip's efforts. In addition, Jim was available to converse and show interest in Philip's studies without taking over or correcting his work. Jim lost many battles, but ultimately he won the war because Phillip eventually took control of his responsibilities, Jim's original goal.

When this homework power struggle started, one of the red flags was that Jim had more interest and investment in Philip's studies than his son did. Whenever the parent has more invested than the child, it's fertile ground for a power struggle to grow and blossom. Instead, parents need to cultivate and nurture the child's interest while stating their expectations along the way.

The situation between Philip and his dad is "a worst case scenario," but if you find yourself in a similar struggle with your child, maybe you can learn from Jim and Philip's situation and end it before it gets out of hand.

Parental Growing Pains

We all wish we could parent with 100% accurate instincts. However, all of us come to parenting with no experience and learn by trial and error. For parents, there's no other way; we will make mistakes and we will learn with each child.

As your children develop and push for autonomy, you'll experience many ups and downs in your relationship with them. Some will involve power struggles. If you had such a power struggle with your boss, you'd probably quit your job; if such a struggle occurred with a neighbor, you might move; if you had a similar struggle with your spouse, you might consider a divorce. But you can't divorce your kids!

Power struggles are the growing pains of relationships. Most adults don't stretch easily, but raising kids requires you to stretch yourself continually in order to find a balance with each child at every stage of development.

When Jim first dropped out of the homework power struggle with Philip, he felt defeated, powerless. But Jim, like all parents, has tremendous power to influence his child in positive ways; each parent just needs to discover where his or her true power lies and tap into it.

10

Tapping into Your True Power

By now you realize that when you are forcefully trying to overpower your child regarding a particular issue, not only do you lose the battle but you're left feeling out of control, powerless, emotional, and exhausted. At these times, you may wonder, "Where does my true power as a parent lie?"

When you clearly lose a power struggle, like Jim who lost the homework battle of wills with his son Philip, you're left wondering, "How could I have avoided this power struggle in the first place?"

In this chapter, you will see how Jim could have avoided the homework power struggle while guiding his son to completing homework assignments responsibly. You will also learn six ways to use your parental power positively to influence and guide your children effectively.

How the Homework Power Struggle Might Have Been Avoided

Jim wondered what he could have done to have avoided the struggle with Philip. How could he have positively influenced his son toward constructive homework habits without engaging in an emotional battle of wills day after day?

To have avoided the power struggle, Jim first would have needed to define his goal, which was to guide Philip toward responsible homework habits while helping him gradually achieve academic competency and independence.

The most useful technique in such situations is called shaping. Parents shape behavior by teaching a skill in baby steps with a great deal of positive reinforcement along the way. (See Chapter 7.)

Looking back, Jim wished he had simply recognized the importance of showing low-key, supportive interest in Philip's assignments. He wished he had said at first, "Let me see the work you need to complete tonight. Looks like you have some arithmetic and spelling." He now knows the importance of offering choices. "Do you want to do your homework after school or after dinner? Do you want to do it at the kitchen table or in your bedroom?" "Okay, you want to do it at the kitchen table after dinner—that's just fine."

Jim didn't realize the value of just sitting quietly near Philip, using proximity control. He could have said, "I've got some work of my own. I'll sit by you at the table; that way if you need any help, I'll be right here." As the two sat down to do their work, Jim could have shown interest in Philip's assignments without taking over. Jim didn't know that his presence and low-key attention would have been his best tools to help Philip on the road to responsible completion of his homework assignments.

If Philip had resisted doing his assignments at his chosen time and place, Jim would have had to adopt a confident stance, exerting power with his presence, voice, and body language, and insisting he get started with a statement regarding the family's values, "In this family academics come first. Your homework is your most important responsibility." Then, once Philip actually did sit down to work on his assignments, it would have been important for Jim to switch to a nurturing approach, exhibiting interest, help, and his calm physical presence.

In addition, at appropriate moments, Dad could also have inserted some statements regarding his expectations, such as, "You know, your school work is important. You're smart—I expect you to work toward excellence."

During the early elementary years, it would have been fine, once Philip had completed his homework each evening, for Dad to ask if Philip would like him to look over his work. Dad could have commented this way, noticing what Philip did that was correct, "I see you've done exactly as your teacher asked. You've spelled all your words correctly and finished your math problems. Good for you." Then he could ask Philip to complete one more step leading to the goal.

"But I see two incorrect answers. Come on, try these again, I know you can get them right. I'll help you if you like." Dad would need to be sensitive here. If Philip resisted and wanted to have the teacher correct his work, then Dad would need to back off temporarily. He might say, "Okay, Philip, I'd like to see you tackle those problems again, but it's your school work; it really is between you and your teacher." With this approach, Dad would have confidently turned the controls and responsibility over to Philip. With Dad backing off, the likelihood is great that Philip would look at those two arithmetic problems again. Better yet, Dad would have skillfully avoided a power struggle, while continuing to influence his son toward homework competency and independence. And the father-son relationship would have stayed intact.

Parents frequently solve problems for their children by simply telling them what to do. A better approach is to explain your problem-solving process by thinking aloud. By doing so, children learn from you how you went about coming to a conclusion. "I see you've finished your homework. So, let's think about this. Here are your notebook and textbooks. If you leave them here, they will be in the way when it's time for breakfast. So what I'd suggest is to put them in your backpack now and set it by the door. Then it will be right there when it's time to get out the door in the morning."

As Philip progressed in school, it would have been better for Jim to gradually withdraw his support, expecting Philip to reach total homework independence by fifth or sixth grade. Parents always need to show interest and offer ideas for whatever their children are involved in, but it's important for the child to gain confidence as he slowly takes on more responsibility for his own homework.

To have been successful, Jim would have also needed to see Philip as a unique individual different from himself. Expecting Philip to succeed in exactly the same way he did was unfair and unrealistic. Although Jim could state his expectations for academic achievement and guide Philip toward that goal, he needed to realize that Philip had to find his own unique approach and style for managing his academic responsibilities.

Unfortunately, Jim didn't proceed in this more effective manner, so a power struggle ensued. Truly, what you don't want is for your child to say at some point in his life, "You know, I actually wanted to do my homework and be a good student, but my dad made such a big deal about doing it his way, I had to prove myself by doing exactly the opposite of what he wanted." Just realize that in parenting, anything you make too much of often has a negative impact on your children.

Tap into Your Positive Power

You do have power as a parent, tremendous power to influence, guide, and teach your children. Rather than attempting to control your children by winning a power struggle, use the following six methods, which are a much more effective use of your real parenting power.

Focus on the positive. Rather than getting into power struggles with your child by constantly pointing what she does wrong, tap into your positive power by noticing and talking about what she does right.

Your daughter, age five, is putting together a jigsaw puzzle. She's completed half of the puzzle, but her interest is fading. Here you have the opportunity to take a negative or positive approach.

Negative: "Aren't you going to finish that puzzle? Why can't you ever finish anything? You're just a quitter." You might say this thinking it will motivate her to finish the task. Unfortunately, such statements leave children paralyzed and often become a self-fulfilling prophecy.

Positive: "Look at you, you completed half of this puzzle. Good for you! Do you want to take a break and finish it later, or do you want me to work with you and finish it now?"

Your preschooler is learning to dress herself. She's completely dressed except for her shoes. Rather than call attention to the shoes, notice what she has accomplished and then prompt her onto the next step to complete the task. "I see you're all dressed: you have your underwear on, your shirt, pants, and socks. Good for you." Now gently prompt your child onto the next step, "Be sure to put your shoes on before we climb in the car."

There's no need to go overboard with praise: "You're so great, you're so wonderful." Instead, precisely describe in a nonjudgmental fashion any behavior you wish to see more of or any action you appreciate. Saying, "I noticed you finished all your homework, good for you," is more meaningful than saying, "You're such a great kid for doing your homework."

Provide proximity control. To get your child to do what you want him to do, you might try talking, reasoning, or explaining your child into compliance. If your child doesn't do as asked, your emotional thermometer might rise to an angry level. Once your anger escalates, the contagious effect of anger takes hold and your child may get angry too. Often an emotional battle ensues.

Rather than a direct, forceful method, realize that

your presence, interest, and involvement provide tremendous subtle control. Trust the fact that your sincere interest and low-key involvement have tremendous power toward influencing your child to appropriate behavior; often words aren't necessary. Physically moving toward your child is a powerful, yet subtle, way to establish or maintain control.

Let's say your child needs to make a card for Grandma's birthday. Get out the paper and markers and sit by your child until the task is completed. As she works, don't prompt or criticize, just watch her and comment positively, "Look at those flowers you're drawing. I love flowers." Your presence and interest keep your child on task.

Let's say you hear your children yelling at one another over who's sitting where for television time. By just moving into proximity of the feuding parties, you can often defuse the battle. You're right there to step in if the disagreement turns physical with hitting or shoving, but usually your calm presence miraculously lowers the antagonism between the two. If they appeal to you to settle the disagreement, you can respond with, "I trust the two of you to resolve the problem without me getting involved." If they reach a stalemate or the battle heats up, you can step in to settle or negotiate the dispute to resolution.

Love and set limits simultaneously. Occasionally when a situation involves your values, or your child's health or safety, you must take a determined, powerful stance. You might say, "I'm telling you 'no,' and it's just because I'm the parent and I said so." Subsequently, a verbal battle between you and your child might result.

Instead, hold on, just communicate that your decision results from love for your child, not out of a personal need to control him. When you hold on to your power, express your love as you draw that line in the parenting sand.

You might say to your two-year-old, "I can't allow you to run away from me in the parking lot. I know you love to play chase and peek-a-boo, but I'm going to carry you into the store to keep you safe, even if you scream and squirm. I'm not carrying you because I must control your every action, but because I love you so much. I must control you and keep you safe until you can control yourself."

You may or may not actually say these words aloud, but at least think them to yourself. This self-talk will prompt you to check yourself and make sure your impulse to control really does spring from love and the best interest of your child.

You might say to your eight-year-old, "I can't allow you to watch that movie. The recreational violence in it isn't healthy for you to see. It's not because I want to control every aspect of your life, I know I can't do that, but I love you enough to protect you from harmful influences."

Impart your values. Many power struggles between parents and their children occur when children don't seem to be adhering to the values of their parents. Forcing values on children only produces power struggles, so don't resort to shoving your values down your children's throats. Instead, realize you have the power to set your children on the path to using their time and interest in the areas that you yourself value most with a subtle, low-key, yet determined approach.

Project ahead to the time when your children are young adults: what do you hope their interests will be? Would you like them involved in academics, sports, organized religion, reading, cooking?

Take reading as an example. How do you go about creating children who choose to read? First of all, it's essential to read yourself. If you want your children to pursue a goal, it's crucial to model that behavior yourself. If reading is a priority, you'll naturally spend your time focused on it. How you use your time underlines your values to your children.

In addition to reading yourself, read to your children, and take them to the library and bookstore. Create positive associations with the reading process; surround your children with love as you read to them. As your children learn to read and stumble across words, don't pressure them for a perfect performance; be patient as you coach them to reading competency. Without lecturing, point out the benefits of reading. "I'm never bored because I always have a book," and "I know about the Civil War from reading *Gone With the Wind*."

You might impose a rule: In our family, there's no television, telephone, or extracurricular activities between 7 and 8 p.m. weekdays. It's the designated time for homework or quiet reading.

To families who read, it's more than just a leisure activity; it lays the foundation for intellectual pursuits, it teaches about history and current events, and helps create interesting, knowledgeable individuals. These long-term benefits of reading are what parents who truly value reading wish to pass on to their children.

You can take the same steps to instill values on religion, family time, sports—whatever you hold dear. Parents hold this power.

Instill virtues. If you realize your fifth grade daughter isn't as polite as you'd like, you might demand she use "thank you," "you're welcome" and "please" more often. By making such a demand, you might enter into a politeness tug-o-war you can't win.

Please understand that you can't force your child into being polite, kind, responsible, or honest, but you have tremendous power to instill these virtues in your children positively, thus developing their character.

When your children are little, envision the qualities you would like them to display eventually. Some might include politeness, integrity, compassion, and self-reliance. Here are some ways to go about instilling these virtues.

When you see someone display a virtue you admire, point it out. Here's integrity: "Jason (the neighbor boy) found a $10.00 bill on our driveway and brought it right in to me. That shows integrity." When your children exhibit a virtue, reinforce it by noticing it and commenting on it. You walk into the kitchen and you see your older son placing a bandage on his brother's bloody knee. Seize the opportunity to describe compassion, "How compassionate, your brother is hurt and you're helping him."

And when you see your children display vices—cheating, lying, or stealing—take the same approach, but in the negative, "I saw you steal a dollar from your sister's purse. Stealing is wrong. I'm disappointed in you. Put the money back and apologize to your sister. If you need money, I'll give you a job so you can earn it."

Modeling the virtues you value is essential, but it's even better if you go one step further by reinforcing your actions with words, "I'm taking Mrs. Cunningham a casserole. She had surgery last week and I wanted to do something kind for her." This is not bragging, it's describing and explaining a virtue you value and exhibit.

Also, keep your parenting antenna alert for stories in the newspaper, on television, and in your everyday life that illustrate the virtues you admire or the vices you abhor. You can even use gossip. If your niece skipped school, use this incident as an opportunity to point out the dishonesty involved in sneaking away from school and the short- and long-term repercussions of that behavior.

You have the power to intentionally develop in your children the virtues you admire. Don't overpower your children in your attempts, just keep at them in a low-key, determined manner.

State your expectations. Too often parents expect certain behaviors from children without informing them of those expectations. Then, when children's behavior falls short of those expected yet uncommunicated expectations, parents feel frustrated, angry, and ineffective. Power struggles sometimes result. By not letting your children know what you expect, you set yourself up for disappointment and your children up for failure.

Instead, realize the importance of stating your expectations ahead of time, which is a much more effective use of your parenting power. All that's required is to clearly communicate to your children what you expect. When you leave to go to a friend's house for dinner, tell your children you expect them to say "Please" and "Thank you," and not run around their friend's house. When it comes to academics, tell your children you expect them to complete their homework assignments. Regarding personal responsibilities, tell your children you expect them to keep track of their belongings and clean up after themselves.

When letting your children know what you expect, make sure your expectations are appropriate for their age and development. For example, expecting your preschooler to sit quietly for an hour-long service at church is unrealistic.

It's a good rule of thumb to review your expectations with your young children just before whatever activity you have planned. If you get into the habit of verbalizing your expectations, your children will learn and display them more quickly. But don't bombard your child with too many expectations at once. Limit them to one or two at a time, "You're going on a 5-mile-bike ride. I expect you'll all stay together and call home when you reach the park."

Last, make it clear by your words and attitudes that although you expect your child to learn to use the toilet, do homework, or dress appropriately for different occasions, none of these is an issue of love. You may be disappointed in your children's behavior from time to time, but you always love them. Isn't this true?

The better your relationship with your child, the less likely you'll engage in a power struggle, and the better the chances your children will stay open to your influence. Don't assume that a loving and liking relationship with your child is a given. Work on it daily. Also, if you've been in a power struggle with your child, you must do all you can to rebuild your relationship. There are specific ways to do this.

11

Rebuilding Damaged Relationships

A prolonged battle of wills between parent and child causes your overall relationship with your child to suffer. You might feel you don't really like your child and your child may avoid you. So, whether your power struggle was short-lived or long-term, once it ends, it's in the best interest of all parties to do all you can to rebuild the parent-child relationship. As the parent, it's your responsibility to take charge of the process.

When a power struggle ends, you may be reluctant to upset the disciplinary apple cart, and so indulge your child: buy toys, go on outings, and ease up on expectations for chores, courtesy, and academic responsibilities. A better approach is two-fold: focus on what your child does that's appropriate, noticing and calling quiet attention to his developing competencies, as well as letting him know you love him just because he exists.

Children are always in the process of developing competencies. Whether learning to use the toilet, read, or jump rope, your child needs you to stand by and cheer her on with interest and encouragement. At the same time, your child needs to know that if she never learned to use the toilet, read, or jump rope, you would love her just the same, that accomplishments are not an issue of love. The nurturing parent knows how to strike this balance.

The more you build your relationship with your child, the more you will see these three benefits: 1) your child is usually more willing to comply with your reasonable requests, 2) if you do get into a power struggle, it is usually short-lived and your relationship recovers quickly; you have a huge reservoir of positive rapport established between you and your child which sustains you through the battle and, 3) you remain a positive, powerful influence in the life of your child. Your children need parents so much; parents are the most important people in their lives. You have the power to establish and rebuild, when necessary, a positive relationship with your child.

Communicating Unconditional Love

Unconditional love is a powerful relationship mender. It tells your child that you love her because she exists. It is love that is not based on anything except existence, not appearance, behavior, achievement, talent, competency, or anything else. There are many ways to express unconditional love.

Say, "I love you," with words and gentle touches. Come right out and say, "I love you. I'm glad you're my kid." It's true, so why not say it? Also communicate your love with hugs and caresses. Anytime you put your child on your lap, you express love without saying a word. As children get older, that lap time will diminish. Older children still need touch; hugs, back scratching, and massage are alternatives they will likely accept.

Focus on your child with eye contact and loving looks. When your child talks, turn, listen, and pay attention to what he says. When you establish eye contact, you prove that you're interested in what he has to say and that he's important to you. Other times, just focus on your child with admiration; look at him, smile, and show love in your eyes. Simply watching with a loving eye demonstrates love.

Complete the cycle of the conversation. When your child says, "Shh, my dolly's sleeping," say, "Okay, I'll be quiet. How long do you think she'll sleep?"

When your daughter comes home from school and says, "My team won at recess today," don't respond with, "Uh-huh," or, "When are you planning to do your homework?" Instead, complete the cycle of the conversation by asking a question, "What were you playing? What was the score?" Your questions prove you heard what your child said, that you're interested, and you want to know more.

Enter into your child's activities, following his lead. If your son is building with Legos®, sit down and build too. Don't make your project better than his. Instead, copy his or create one of similar complexity. When you enter into your child's activities, the focus is on building the relationship, not on using the time for competition or instruction.

Notice when your children come and go. When your daughter comes home from school, greet her with a simple, "I'm glad you're home." As she heads out the door to play, lovingly inquire, "Where are you going and when will you be back?"

Children need to know their presence and absence make a difference. Such inquiry is an easy and commonplace way to show you care. You give your child the message that "In our family, we all keep track of one another." If well instilled when children are young, this message pays off during the teen years when it's even more important to keep track of kids' whereabouts.

Engage in a mutually enjoyable activity that's of particular interest to the child. It could be cooking, building a model, going to the movies, or participating in a sport.

Janet was never interested in athletics, but her young son loved playing and watching sports. To connect with her son, Janet cultivated, even faked at times, an interest in sports for the sake of maintaining a relationship with her son. If they had a disagreement, it was forgotten once the beloved basketball team took the floor or the baseball players ran onto the field.

Accept children's feelings. Feelings are neither right nor wrong, they just occur; when accepted and understood, they resolve. When you empathize by saying, "I know you're jealous of your baby sister," you communicate an understanding which comes across to the child as love. Be indulgent when it comes to accepting your child's feelings; however, curb any accompanying negative behavior. "It's frustrating having a baby brother who cries, but I can't allow you to pinch him."

Help children out. In parenting, one basic rule of thumb is this: Don't do for children what they can do for themselves. However, when a child is emotional, it's okay to step in and help out. If your child is late for the bus and can't find his back pack, go ahead and help him out. Be careful not to make this situation into a daily routine, just realize that such help conveys love. If your child has a school project requiring clay, cardboard, and wire, help him locate the materials he needs.

Along with Love Goes Teaching Skills

Now that we have looked at ways to convey your unconditional love, be sure to balance that affection with recognition and support for your children's efforts to build their competencies. If you go overboard expressing and demonstrating unwavering love without requiring your child to develop into a competent human being, you risk creating a little prince or princess who believes all he or she does is darling and wonderful, even when demonstrating little self-control or responsibility. The following are ways to promote and prompt your child into developing into a competent, responsible person who works to reach his potential.

Notice and talk about what your child does that's appropriate. "I noticed you finished your math assignment—good for you." Noticing and describing are more meaningful to children than judging their behavior. Saying, "I see you put all the blocks in the red bin" is more meaningful than stating, "Good job." Precisely describing your child's positive actions says you took time to notice exactly what the child did right.

The power of your words encourages the behavior to continue and even improve. When you wish further compliance, describe what your child is doing appropriately at the moment, and then make a request that requires additional compliance. "You set the table. Thanks. Now please put the napkins on."

Notice small steps toward competency, but don't expect or insist on perfection. Some parents overlook progress made and are always pointing out how a child can do more or better. This is discouraging for the child.

Whether your child is learning to tidy his bedroom or complete a homework task, call attention to each small step toward the goal. "You're learning to write your name. I see you even know to capitalize the first letter." "You can spell eight of your spelling words. Way to go!" "The Legos® are cleaned up off your bedroom floor. Thanks." As your child works toward competency, cheer her on with encouraging words like, "Way to go," "Good for you," and "I'm proud of you and I'll bet you're proud of yourself, too."

Watch your child with a loving, approving expression as she works toward competency. Remember how you watched as your child first learned to walk? Your child needs to see that same look of adoration in your eyes as she learns to read, ride a bicycle, or thank Grandma politely for a birthday gift. As your seven-year-old learns to roller skate, provide support and show interest by simply watching him practice.

Be your child's mentor as she strives for success. If your child is working on a science fair project and wants your help, do so, but don't take over. The parent's role is to help out, but only as far as needed. You want the project to be your child's success, not your's. If your child is interested in trains, you might take her to the library for books, plan a train ride, or visit a train museum. Support her interest, don't dominate it.

Let your child help. Toddlers copy as you cook, clean, and use the computer. They want to do what you do, be right by your side. They think they're helping, but as every parent knows, their help really isn't much help at all. Nevertheless, it's important to involve them in what you do, because when you do, it makes them feel capable and encourages them to develop their competencies further. Preschoolers also like to help: they can set the table, feed the dog, or assist you in making cookies. You can probably do all these things better and faster by yourself, but don't. Involve them, demonstrate how to go about each task, and praise their efforts. They're eager helpers, especially when they're involved with you.

School-aged kids can be hard working. They immerse themselves in hobbies, projects, and tasks that truly contribute to the household, school, and even the community. Encourage and support such industry. If they develop a skill that's beyond you, let them demonstrate it or teach you how to do it.

Say "No" and set limits. Don't ever believe that setting reasonable limits appropriate to your child's age and development is detrimental to your relationship with your child. Letting children know what you expect, telling them clearly what you will and will not allow, provides emotional safety for children. Every child feels secure knowing a loving parent will step in and keep him in line.

Limit criticism. Your five-year-old child wants to wrap a package for her friend's birthday. She works hard, using too much tape and not enough paper. It's not an artistic wrap, but she's proud of it. It's not your job to point out the errors in her wrapping technique. Let it be. If wrapping is a skill you want her to be proficient in, next time you wrap a present, show her how you do it. Or if she starts to wrap a package another day, get her started by showing her how to cut the paper so it covers the entire box. If you quickly point out what's wrong with her job, especially when she is perfectly proud of her work, you take the wind out of her competency sails. There's no need to deflate those sails after the fact; that's simply criticism. If you wait for the next time the child starts up a similar activity, then your instruction will be better received and more useful to the child. That's teaching, not criticism. Realize the main difference between criticism and teaching is timing.

When your child exhibits a behavior or a virtue you wish to reinforce, describe the action and attach the appropriate label. Here's how: you go to church weekly, but your spouse chooses to stay home. Attending services is a value you hold dear. Your child goes willingly with you each Sunday, so state your appreciation, "I really like going to church together with you. It's my favorite part of the week." Let's say your son breaks your neighbor's window playing baseball. He comes to you with the truth. Tell him he will need to pay for the window with his own money, but what you appreciate most about his behavior is that he came to you with the truth. Tell your child what you like, appreciate, and admire; tell your child what brings you pride. Then your child will like, appreciate, and admire himself when he exhibits those virtues.

Again, remember to strike a good balance. If you focus only on your child's achievements, you create a child who is either an overachiever or an underachiever. The overachiever believes that if he gets straight A's, is captain of the soccer team, and winner of the spelling bee, then he'll be loved and adored by you. The underachiever is the child who realizes he'll never live up to his parents' expectations because his parents are always there to point out how he could have accomplished the task better or done more; he gives up. His inner voice says, "Why try when I never get it right?" This is why it's so important to balance your messages between unconditional love and support for developing competencies.

You probably already adhere to some of these suggestions. Notice which ones you do and congratulate yourself. Then pick out more to work into your parenting repertoire. Not only do these tips build your relationship with your child and help to rebuild it after a power struggle, all of these help prevent power struggles from occurring in the first place. In addition, they build your child's self-esteem; she learns to see herself as lovable when she receives unconditional love and capable as she achieves competency. When you treat your child thus, she learns to treat others in the same fashion.

The way you treat your child will affect you too; you will feel better in your role as a nurturing parent. Any guilt you may feel will diminish and your parenting self-esteem will soar. A loving, healthy relationship between you and your child will have a positive effect on your entire household.

Afterword

Children need powerful, nurturing parents who decisively or intuitively know when to hold on to their power and control, when and how to gradually let up on controls, and when to drop out, allowing the child to grasp the controls of a particular situation.

Truly, for some parents and children, power struggles seldom occur. The child who is born with a fairly easy temperament and the parent who intuitively knows how to gradually let up on controls may never engage in an emotional battle with one another. For other parents and children, there may be many tug-o-wars as the child bulldozes his or her way to independence, or as the parent fights relinquishing the control he or she feels necessary for appropriate guidance and discipline.

By now you realize that parents who engage in emotional battles with their children, dominating and attempting to control their every move, not only destroy the parent-child relationship, they lose the ability to influence their child in positive ways.

If you're a parent who finds herself or himself occasionally or frequently in power struggles with one or all of your children, you now have some information, understanding, and options for resolving those power struggles. You realize that power struggles destroy the parent-child relationship, and you, the responsible, loving parent, will do all you can to bring the power struggle to a peaceful resolution for the sake of your child.

For domestic tranquility, your parent-child relationship, and having positive influence over your child, do all you can to end any emotional battle of wills. This book is not about winning or losing one of these battles, it's about doing what's best for your child through love and positive guidance.

Helpful Resources

Crary, Elizabeth. *Pick Up Your Socks . . . and Other Skills Growing Children Need! A Practical Guide to Raising Responsible Children.* Seattle: Parenting Press, Inc. 1990.

Power struggles often occur because parents don't have realistic expectations for their children's behavior. This book gives step-by-step guidelines for teaching responsibility appropriate to a child's age and abilities.

Faber, Adele and Mazlish, Elaine. *Siblings Without Rivalry: How to Help Your Children Live Together So You Can Live Too.* New York: W.W. Norton & Company, Inc. 1987.

Power struggles occur between siblings as well as between parent and child. The authors offer many strategies for reducing the occurrence of sibling fighting and rivalry.

Faull, Jan. *Mommy, I Have to Go Potty!* Seattle: Raefield-Roberts, Publishers and Parenting Press, Inc. 1995.

When parents get into potty training power struggles with their children, they lose because ultimate control lies with the children. This book offers many approaches to potty training and includes a chapter on ending potty training power struggles.

Gottman, John. *The Heart of Parenting: Raising an Emotionally Intelligent Child.* New York: Simon & Schuster 1997.

No parent can control a child's emotions. If tried, power struggles result; emotions intensify. This book helps parents understand their roles as emotion coaches, nurturing emotional development and strength.

Heath, Harriet. *Using Your Values to Raise Your Child to Be an Adult You Admire.* Seattle: Parenting Press, Inc. 2000.

Parents have the power to instill their values in their children, raise children with admirable virtues and strong character. This practical book shows parents how to do so in a steady, low-key intentional way, without power struggles.

Kurchinka, Mary Sheedy. *Kids, Parents, and Power Struggles: Winning for a Lifetime.* New York: HarperCollins 2000.

This book offers a completely different approach to reducing the chance of power struggles. It provides suggestions for avoiding conflicts and managing them, chiefly by understanding the emotions that fuel them.

Nelson, Jane, Cheryl Erwin, and Roslyn Duffy. *Positive Discipline for Preschoolers.* Rocklin, Calif.: Prima Publishing 1999.

Every parent needs a reference for discipline. With good disciplinary tools at your fingertips, the likelihood of power struggles diminishes. This book is one of a series of books on positive discipline that goes through the teenage years.

Rosenberg, Marshall. *Nonviolent Communication: A Language of Compassion.* Del Mar, Calif.: PuddleDancer Press 1999.

At the heart of parenting lies loving communication. Words can build relationships or tear them apart. Hurtful language seeps into most power struggles. This book teaches compassionate communication techniques that transfer from parent to child.

Samalin, Nancy. *Love and Anger: The Parental Dilemma.* New York: Viking 1991.

Anger between parent and child escalates along with power struggles. To end a power struggle, parents need a plan and a matter-of-fact attitude. This book helps parents understand that perplexing emotion, anger.

Steelsmith, Shari. Go to Your Room! Consequences That Teach. Seattle: Raefield-Roberts, Publishers and Parenting Press, Inc. 2000.

Sound disciplinary techniques at one's fingertips are the best deterrent for power struggles. This book clarifies the use of consequences and offers many specific consequences parents have found helpful.

Index

Skill-building Books for Thoughtful Parents

Without Spanking or Spoiling: A Practical Approach to Toddler and Preschool Guidance by Elizabeth Crary, M.S. takes the best ideas from four major child guidance approaches and combines them into one practical resource guide. A classic book loved by parents for 20 years. Useful with ages birth to 6 years. 112 pages, $14.95 paper, $19.95 library binding

Time-In: When Time-Out Doesn't Work by Jean Illsley Clarke, M.A. is for every parent who has felt frustrated, helpless, angry, or scared when traditional parenting tools don't work. Winner of a *Parents' Choice* Approval Award. Useful with ages 2 through 12 years. 80 pages, $9.95 paper, $18.95 library binding

Using Your Values to Raise Your Child to Be an Adult You Admire by Harriet Heath, Ph.D. shows parents how to use their own values as the base for everyday parenting decisions, with an eye to the long-term growth of their children. Winner of a *Parenting Resources Gold Award.* Useful with ages birth to 20 years. 178 pages, $16.95 paper, $19.95 library binding

Grounded for Life?! Stop Blowing Your Fuse and Start Communicating with Your Teenager by Louise F. Tracy, M.S. shows parents of kids 12 to 18 how to keep lines of communication open and clear, with responsibility for behavior placed where it belongs. Unique blend of professional experience as a middle-school counselor and motherhood of six former teenagers. Winner of a *Parents' Choice* Approval Award. 164 pages, $12.95 paper, $19.95 library binding

Parenting Press, Inc.
Dept. 203, P.O. Box 75267
Seattle, Washington 98125
Toll free 1-800-992-6657

In Canada, call Raincoast Books
Distribution Company,
1-800-663-5714
Prices subject to change without notice